Le Corbeau

CINÉ-FILES: The French Film Guides
Series Editor: Ginette Vincendeau

From the pioneering days of the Lumière brothers' Cinématographe in 1895, France has been home to perhaps the most consistently vibrant film culture in the world, producing world-class directors and stars, and a stream of remarkable movies, from popular genre films to cult avant-garde works. Many of these have found a devoted audience outside France, and the arrival of DVD is now enabling a whole new generation to have access to contemporary titles as well as the great classics of the past.

The Ciné-Files French Film Guides build on this welcome new access, offering authoritative and entertaining guides to some of the most significant titles, from the silent era to the early twenty-first century. Written by experts in French cinema, the books combine extensive research with the author's distinctive, sometimes provocative perspective on each film. The series will thus build up an essential collection on great French classics, enabling students, teachers and lovers of French cinema both to learn more about their favourite films and make new discoveries in one of the world's richest bodies of cinematic work.

Ginette Vincendeau

Published Ciné-Files
Alphaville (Jean-Luc Godard, 1965) – Chris Darke
Les Diaboliques (Henri-Georges Clouzot, 1955) – Susan Hayward
La Haine (Mathieu Kassovitz, 1995) – Ginette Vincendeau
La Reine Margot (Patrice Chéreau, 1994) – Julianne Pidduck

Forthcoming Ciné-Files include:
Amélie (Jean-Pierre Jeunet, 2001) – Isabelle Vanderschelden
Le Corbeau (Henri-Georges Clouzot, 1943) – Judith Mayne
Casque d'or (Jacques Becker, 1952) – Sarah Leahy
Cléo de 5 à 7 (Agnès Varda, 1961) – Valerie Orpen
La Règle du jeu (Jean Renoir, 1939) – Keith Reader
Rififi (Jules Dassin, 1955) – Alastair Phillips
La Grande illusion (Jean Renoir, 1937) – Martin O'Shaughnessy
Un chien andalou (Luis Buñuel, 1929) – Elza Adamowicz
À bout de souffle (Jean-Luc Godard, 1960) – Ramona Fotiade

Le Corbeau

(Henri-Georges Clouzot, 1943)

Judith Mayne

I.B. TAURIS

LONDON · NEW YORK

Published in 2007 by I.B.Tauris & Co. Ltd

6 Salem Road, London W2 4BU

175 Fifth Avenue, New York NY 10010

ibtauris.com

ISBN: 978 1 84511 370 4

A full CIP record for this book is available from the British Library

Typeset in Minion by Dexter Haven Associates Ltd, London
Printed and bound in Great Britain by TJ International Ltd, Padstow, Cornwall

Contents

Acknowledgements

Thank you to the Departments of French & Italian and Women's Studies, and the College of Humanities, at Ohio State University for continued research support, and to my research assistant, Clarissa Moore. I am particularly indebted to these individuals in the Archives section of the Bibliothèque du Film (BIFI) in Paris: Valdo Kneubhüler, Karine Mauduit, Régis Robert, Nadine Tenèze and Delphine Warin. A special thanks to Ginette Vincendeau for inviting me to participate in the series. I am grateful to Florian Loubard and Kevin Snorteland for their acute observations about *Le Corbeau*. As always, thanks to Terry Moore.[1]

Note

1 Portions of Chapter Two are adapted from my essay 'Henri-Georges Clouzot's Le Corbeau and the Crimes of Women', *Sites: Journal of 20th Century French Studies* 4 (2000), pp. 319–341.

Synopsis

Le Corbeau tells the story of a fictional town, Saint-Robin – 'here or elsewhere', as the opening title of the film informs us – deluged with anonymous letters. Dr Rémy Germain, a relatively recent resident of the town, is a particular target of the letters. The first letter we see is addressed to Dr Germain, and accuses him of having an affair with Laura Vorzet (Micheline Francey), the wife of a local psychiatrist. Early scenes in the film establish a number of suspicions – that Dr Germain performs abortions; that Marie Corbin, a nurse at the hospital and the sister of Laura, is stealing drugs and is consumed with jealousy over her perception that her sister is carrying on an affair with Dr Germain; that Dr Germain is genuinely attracted to Laura Vorzet; and that Denise Saillens, who lives in the same building as Dr Germain, fakes illness to lure him into bed. Suspicious characters, particularly women, seem to abound in the film, from Marie Corbin, who is a busybody, to Rolande, the 14-year-old niece of Denise, who peeks through keyholes.

The anonymous letters increase in number, reaching epidemic proportions, and they reveal increasingly scandalous information about financial misdeeds, adulterous affairs and general misbehaviour. When a cancer patient in the hospital kills himself after receiving a letter telling him that his disease is fatal, suspicions turn to the nurse Marie Corbin, who is pursued by an angry mob. But, after she is arrested and put into prison, another letter appears, floating down from a church balcony during mass. Suspicion turns to Dr Germain, since he is mentioned in virtually all of the letters. As enquiries into Germain's life are mounted, Dr Germain's own past is revealed: he was a famous brain surgeon, whose wife was expecting a child, and the doctor who treated her allowed both her and the child to die. Hence in his new life in Saint-Robin, Germain – now a general practitioner rather than a surgeon – always makes the choice to save the mother's life, and hence the accusations of abortion.

Eventually it is agreed that the culprit must be one of the parishioners seated in the church balcony when the letter drifted down, and they are subjected to a lengthy dictation session in order to weed out the guilty party. Dr Vorzet presides, as he is a self-described expert in *l'anonymographie*, the study of anonymous letters and handwriting analysis. Denise faints during the session, thus pointing to her potential guilt, yet the results of her handwriting are inconclusive. Dr Germain visits her, and discovers an anonymous letter addressed to him, announcing that Denise is pregnant. Thinking he has discovered the source of the anonymous letters, Dr Germain confronts Denise, who admits only to having written this one letter. But, she says, Laura had telephoned her earlier to tell her of a particularly nasty and threatening letter she had just received. Germain goes to Laura, who denies knowledge of the letter. But, until Germain discovers ink marks on Laura's hands, he thinks he has been had by Denise. Dr Vorzet intervenes, tells Germain that he has just discovered Laura's guilt, and accepts Germain's offer to declare her insane. Rejoined with Denise, Germain describes Laura's guilt, but Denise insists that this is not possible. Germain returns to the Vorzet house after Laura has been taken away, and finds Dr Vorzet, collapsed on his desk, murdered as he was writing a final anonymous letter. His throat was slit, and Germain looks through the open window to see the mother of the cancer patient walk away, her revenge enacted.

Introduction

For most of his career in the cinema, from the 1930s, when he began work as a screenwriter, to his last film as a director, *La Prisonnière/The Prisoner* in 1968, Henri-Georges Clouzot seemed a bit out of touch and out of time. Two of his films from the 1950s, *Le Salaire de la peur/Wages of Fear* (1953) and *Les Diaboliques/The Fiends* (1955), are recognised as classics of French cinema.[1] But, in the context of the 1950s, Clouzot's work fits neither of the categories that have long been considered representative of the era, the 'tradition of quality' and '*auteur* cinema'. His portrait of Pablo Picasso, *Le Mystère Picasso/The Mystery of Picasso* (1956), is widely recognised as a brilliant film about art and the artist, but rarely is the film considered as having had much of an influence in the context of French film-making. In the 1960s, Clouzot seemed – like many film-makers of his generation – to be out of touch with the new approaches to film-making that heralded the advent of the New Wave. His last two features, *La Vérité* (*Truth*, 1960) and *La Prisonnière*, might have been interesting in their own right, but Clouzot was considered passé at the time of their release.

For better or worse, Clouzot was very much a man of his time during the period that solidified his reputation as a film-maker. During the Second World War, Clouzot worked for the Nazi-owned film company Continental Films. He wrote two screenplays for films directed by others (*Le Dernier des six/Last of the Six*, 1941, and *Les Inconnus dans la maison/Strangers in the House*, 1942), and directed his first two films (*L'Assassin habite au 21/The Assassin Lives at Number 21*, 1942, and *Le Corbeau/The Raven*, 1943) for Continental. Additionally, after the success of *Le Dernier des six* (one of Continental's earliest releases), Clouzot was hired as the head of the company's screenplay division. Perhaps more than any other French film-maker of the time, Clouzot was closely involved with the workings of

Continental, from requesting script changes, to overseeing what films would be produced, to working closely with Alfred Greven, the head of the company. When France was liberated from German Occupation, *Le Corbeau* became the single film, and Clouzot the single director, that embodied all of the implications of Continental's successes during the war. Clouzot was punished accordingly. Even though his three-year suspension from film-making was less harsh than the punishment accorded others in the cinema (like stage and screen actor, director and writer Sacha Guitry, who was in jail for three years), and certainly mild compared to the death sentence imposed on writer Robert Brasillach, Clouzot's initial banishment from the cinema became a potent symbol of the Second World War and its aftermath.

Indeed, to this day, *Le Corbeau* remains the emblematic film of the Occupation. Other Occupation films, like Marcel Carné's *Les Visiteurs du soir* (1942) or Jean Delannoy's *L'Eternel retour* (1943), have become recognised as classics of French cinema, but they are generally discussed either as films that are successful *despite* the fact that they were made during the Occupation, or as products of an *auteurist* vision that takes them out of their immediate historical context (in the case of Delannoy's film, Jean Cocteau worked so closely on the screenplay that he is often considered as much of an *auteur* as Delannoy was). Significantly, both Carné's and Delannoy's/Cocteau's films evoke a somewhat mythical past (fifteenth-century France and the legend of Tristan and Yseult, respectively). In contrast, Clouzot's film is set in what Jean-Pierre Jeancolas calls the 'contemporain vague' of many Occupation films, a vague yet recognisable present tense unspecified in terms of a moment or place.[2]

If *Le Corbeau* was put on trial (and it was) as a film that was 'anti-French', much of the controversy surrounding the film had to do with Clouzot himself as the film-maker most invested in, and most adept at, cinematic collaboration during the war. According to Clouzot's own account, *Le Corbeau* was not a film that Continental was particularly eager to make, and Clouzot claimed that he was fired from the studio after the film was completed. As with virtually all stories of collaborationist activity during the war, such accounts as these have to be taken with the proverbial grain of salt. Yet as audiences since the 1940s have seen the film, the question remains: how could a film that deals so explicitly with anonymous letters be approved and financed by a Nazi company, given that the Germans depended upon such letters for information about the whereabouts of Jews and members of the Resistance? How could a regime so repressive be so apparently permissive in regard to the cinema, which had high attendance during the war? As Evelyn Ehrlich observes, French Occupation cinema is a cinema of paradox, and *Le Corbeau* exemplifies the peculiar and contradictory aspects of the era.[3] *Le Corbeau* embodies, perhaps more than any other single film, this paradoxical quality of a French film industry that thrived under oppressive conditions, and that produced its share of provocative and engaging films.

Notes

1   For an in-depth discussion of *Les Diaboliques*, see Hayward, Susan, *Les Diaboliques* (London: I.B.Tauris, 2005).

2   Jeancolas, Jean-Pierre, *15 ans d'années trente: Le cinéma des français 1929–1944* (Paris: Stock, 1983), pp. 321–322.

3   Ehrlich, Evelyn, *Cinema of Paradox: French Filmmaking Under the German Occupation* (New York: Columbia University Press, 1985).

1 Production contexts

In the summer of 1940, France was in a state of turmoil, catastrophe and disarray. French military forces had spent months anticipating German attack during the *drôle de guerre*, or 'phoney war', when French armies were assembled near the Maginot Line (from 3 September 1939 to 10 May 1940). When fighting finally broke out, French military forces were defeated quickly by the German aggressor. The armistice was signed on 25 June. Divided into occupied and (euphemistically) non-occupied zones, France was controlled by the German occupiers in the northern zone, and the collaborationist Vichy government, with the First World War veteran Maréchal Pétain its putative head, in the south. In 1942, Germany occupied the entire country, thus erasing the distinction between occupied and non-occupied zones.

Few periods of contemporary history have been so subject to reflection and analysis as these *années noires*, or 'dark years'. The story of France during the Second World War is complex, and understandings of that story have changed over the decades. One such change is the move from a Resistance story to a collaborationist one – that is, from a portrait of France as a heroic anti-fascist country united in its desire to defeat Germany, to a portrait of a deeply divided country suspicious of the Left and far more sympathetic to the forces of the Right than had previously been acknowledged.[1] Within such a context, the story of the fate of French cinema during the war might seem trivial indeed. Because of a series of important developments, the French film industry was able not only to survive, but to thrive, despite the fact that a number of important directors – Julien Duvivier, René Clair, Jean Renoir, to name a few – left the country. As Evelyn Ehrlich observes, '… to those who endured the occupation, the cinema was of great importance. Movie theaters provided refuge from the uncertainty and hardship of everyday life. The French public flocked to the darkened theaters to see a world they had lost or one that existed only in their dreams.'[2]

Henri-Georges Clouzot's 1943 film *Le Corbeau* embodies the status of French cinema during the war, its successes and failures, its limits and its possibilities. To be sure, other films made during the war have achieved the status of masterpieces of French cinema, including Marcel Carné's *Les Visiteurs du soir/The Night Visitors* (1942) and *Les Enfants du paradis/Children of Paradise* (1943–1945). But both these films are set in the past, in the mythical medieval castle of *Les Visiteurs du soir* and on the nineteenth-century Boulevard du Crime in *Les Enfants du paradis*. Many have argued that these films do indeed engage with and reflect upon the reality of an Occupied France. But *Le Corbeau* is so openly and boldly situated in a contemporary context that many have wondered how the film could possibly have been made, particularly given how its subject matter – anonymous letters that poison the atmosphere of a small town – is so directly reflective of Occupied France, where anonymous letters were a common practice encouraged by the Nazis. Despite the fact that its opening title announces that the film is set in a 'petite ville, ici ou ailleurs' ('a little town, here or elsewhere'), the tale of anonymous letters reveals a town in crisis, and a community in turmoil, very much like the France of 1943 when the film was made.

Continental and COIC

The significance of *Le Corbeau* as a film of the Occupation needs to be understood first and foremost in relationship to Continental Films, the German-owned company that produced it. Many companies made films during the Occupation, but Continental dominated the French film industry during the war in both economic and cultural terms. The influence and dominance of Continental suggest a number of interrelated questions. Why were so many French film personnel – directors, actors, technicians – willing to work for a Nazi company (aside from the obvious fact that they needed work)? How did a Nazi company present a public face that was recognisably French? What kind of cinematic presence did Continental promote in France, and how much did Continental 'collaborate' with the French – as opposed to dominating them? How was film understood during the war from the perspectives of both those in the industry and those who attended motion pictures at record levels?

Despite the economic hardships and the realities of invasion and Occupation, French cinema flourished during the Second World War. Continental produced 30 of the 220 fiction films made during the Occupation (more than any other single company).[3] Since Continental was a Nazi company, it comes as little surprise that it was able to acquire the means, the materials and the personnel necessary to dominate the film market. If, as Jacques Siclier claims, everyday filmgoers in France during the war made little distinction between films produced by Continental and those produced by other companies, then this is a surely a sign of Continental's success in demonstrating French collaboration rather than German domination.[4] Continental's films 'looked' French (and in some ways they looked American, as well – none too surprising given that American films were virtually absent during the war, thus giving film-makers the opportunity to compete with the American product). Familiar faces appeared in Continental films, actors like Pierre Fresnay and Fernand Ledoux, actresses like Danielle Darrieux and Ginette Leclerc. Continental's films may well have seemed like any other French film to audiences, but, for those who worked in the film industry, Continental was a brutal reminder of the stakes of German investment in, and domination of, France.

Continental Films was officially created only months after the invasion of France, on 3 October 1940. The significance of Continental was amplified by the creation of another organisation, COIC (Comité d'Organisation de L'Industrie Cinématographique/Committee for the Organisation of the Cinema Industry), administered by the collaborationist Vichy government. In different and inevitably interconnected ways, these two organisations would bring order and regulation to the chaotic French film industry and would shape the contours of French film-making until the end of the war, in the case of Continental, and well beyond, in the case of COIC (the organisation was maintained after the war's end and eventually became the CNC, the Centre National de la Cinématographie/National Cinema Centre, which still exists today).

A number of men had important posts with COIC over the years, including government official Guy de Carmoy, producers Raoul Ploquin and Roger Richebé, and director Louis Daquin. Although the 'face' of Continental may well have been French, a single man successfully created its film empire, the German film producer Alfred Greven. Greven was a veteran of the First World War who had been head of production at UFA (Universum Film Aktiengesellschaft/Universal Film Company) studios as well as the director of Terra Films (the company that produced one of the most vile anti-Semitic films in history, *Jew Süss* [directed by Veit Harlan, 1940]). Greven was a cinephile and a Francophile, described by some as charming and by others as the prototype of an authoritarian Nazi. Maurice Bessy describes Greven as '43 years old, tall, terse, going bald... Dynamic, with good French, friendly but distant.'[5] Although he recruited the best talent he could find for Continental, Greven also exerted considerable (and at times threatening) pressure on individuals to get what he wanted.

One of the most important aspects of Greven's background was that he already had considerable experience in French–German collaboration, since he had worked with some of the French directors, writers and actors who made French/German co-productions in the 1930s, one of whom was Henri-Georges Clouzot. A contemporary observer may well wonder how French directors could so willingly sign up for an Occupation company. Here, the background of 1930s European film production is essential to keep in mind. Many of those who were first hired to work at Continental (actors as well as directors and screenwriters) had participated in the numerous French–German film productions that were common practice in the 1930s. Given the many weaknesses in the French film industry of the 1930s, these films allowed the Nazi film industry to take advantage of lucrative French markets. The films were literally produced twice on the same sets, one version with French actors, another with German actors. Henri Decoin (who would eventually work for Continental), for instance, directed *Le Domino vert* in 1935 in Berlin starring two popular French actors, his then wife Danielle Darrieux and Charles Vanel. The film was produced by the German company UFA and was distributed in France by the German company ACE (Alliance Cinématographique Européene/European Cinematic Alliance). German actors took the place of Darrieux and Vanel for the German version. UFA's producer for the film was Greven, appointed by Joseph Goebbels, the Propaganda Minister for the Third Reich.[6] (The German financial support for these ventures was, of course, Nazi money.) The French producer was Raoul Ploquin, who would eventually become the head of COIC.[7]

Given this history of French–German collaboration, and of Nazi financing of the French film industry, Rémy Pithon concludes that going to work for Continental in 1941 'must not have seemed a novelty to someone who had spent time in the offices of ACE and had signed contracts with UFA in Paris'.[8] Danielle Darrieux, for one, claimed in her autobiography that since she had, like many of her colleagues, worked in Germany in the 1930s, she really didn't have a clear idea of what working for Continental meant. The observation seems disingenuous on Darrieux's part, but she soon discovered what working for Continental entailed. Darrieux and Decoin had separated when they worked together on *Premier rendez-vous*, one of Continental's first films. She became romantically involved with Portofirio Rubirosa, a diplomat from the Dominican Republic whose anti-Nazi sentiments were well known. Greven pressured Darrieux into making two more films for Continental (*Caprices*, 1942, and *La Fausse maîtresse*, 1942) by threatening to make life difficult for Rubirosa. This side of Greven, demonstrating a determination to get what he wanted at any cost, undoubtedly contributed to the image many had of him as an 'ideal Nazi'. When Darrieux refused to make any more films for Continental, Clouzot and director André Cayatte went to see her to put pressure on her, but she continued to refuse. Greven insisted that she become virtually invisible in France, that she make no more films for any company and that no magazines could write about her.[9]

Despite the unpleasant end to his relationship with Darrieux, Greven's acquaintance with so many French directors and actors facilitated the creation of Continental Films. Clouzot's case is typical in the sense that he was part of a talent pool already familiar with and known to the German film industry as well as with producers like Greven. Continental Films had an extremely well-integrated organisation at its disposal, for Greven was a direct link to Tobis (the German production company that also produced many films in France), to UFA, as well as to ACE. ACE distributed all of Continental's films during the war, as well as German films in France. In addition, Greven created SOGEC (Société de gestion et d'exploitation du cinéma/Society for Film Management and Distribution), made possible by the appropriation of French movie theatres owned by Jews. Immediately after the invasion, all movie theatres closed in France and gradually reopened only at the discretion of the Germans. Cinemas owned by Jews were not permitted to reopen, and SOGEC managed to buy large numbers of theatres by virtue of its huge amount of capital and the immediate implementation of anti-Semitic laws. Greven also acquired exclusive access to Paris-Studio-Cinéma for shooting. Greven moved quickly to capitalise on resources, and he had a complete system of production, distribution and exhibition at his disposal, thus creating a virtual film empire.

But perhaps most important, especially in terms of the image that would be projected of Continental Films, Greven was able to hire a group of talented and well-known directors from the outset. Le Film, the official film journal of Vichy, announced in its second issue that five directors had been hired by Continental: Maurice Tourneur, Marcel Carné, Christian-Jaque, Georges Lacombe and Léo Joannon.[10] Carné later described his contract as a bit of trickery on Greven's part, and while the director did indeed have a project in mind for Continental, it was never realised and he was able to extricate himself from his contract.[11] The remaining directors were well known. Christian-Jaque, Léo Joannon and Georges Lacombe had established their directing careers in the 1930s (Joannon had directed one film before 1930), while Maurice Tourneur was a film veteran who had been making films in the US and France since the silent era.

Continental Films dominated the French film industry during the war, and there were conflicts about its authority and presence. From the point of view of the collaborationist Vichy government, the film industry was one of many in France in need of serious overhaul and regulation. Regulation sometimes meant rules that provided much-needed economic boosts to the film industry, such as the abolition of double features (thus immediately raising the profits on individual films), and the successful negotiation of bank loans that provided much-needed capital for film production. But regulation also meant Aryanisation of the film industry. From the point of view of those in the film industry, COIC provided the means to ensure that French cinema would remain French (and sometimes 'French' meant free from German control, while at others it meant free from so-called 'Jewish influence'). While official pronouncements in *Le Film* praised Continental Films and collaboration in general, there were in fact profound conflicts between COIC and Continental in the course of the war, largely because there was never any question as to which organisation really held the power and authority to shape the course of French film history.

COIC was entirely justified in its fears about French cinema. For French film-makers and producers who remained in France during the war, the safeguarding of the cinema was not only a matter of national pride, and not only a way to preserve some part of French culture in the face of defeat and Occupation, but also an attempt to address the problems that had put French cinema of the 1930s on the verge of economic collapse. The Occupation provided an impetus for the development of structures and regulations that virtually all members of the film community agreed were necessary in order to end the financial instability that characterised French cinema of the 1930s.[12]

French films of the 1930s, whether masterpieces of poetic realism like Carné's *Le jour se lève* (1939), innovative explorations of the aesthetic qualities of sound film like René Clair's *Sous les toits de Paris* (1930), or *auteurist* visions like Jean Renoir's *La Grande illusion* (1937), *La Bête humaine* (1938) or *La Règle du jeu/Rules of the Game* (1939), continue to be recognised to this day as marvellous contributions to the art of the cinema. Yet these films were produced in a context of economic and industrial chaos. The costs of film-making rose steadily in the 1930s, and French films were always in a precarious financial state because of the large number of American films that were shown in France, with virtually no quotas or protection of the French film industry. The film industry was not regulated, and it was not uncommon for a company to collapse in ruin after the production of a single film. It was generally agreed that something needed to be done, and in 1937, Popular Front Education Minister Jean Zay declared famously that 'il faut épurer le cinéma français'('French cinema must be purged').[13] Not much was done until the outbreak of the 'phoney war' in September 1939, and then the imposition of government regulation had more to do with censorship (no films that were demoralising; no anti-war films) than with a reorganisation of the industry. Only when the Germans invaded France was Jean Zay's call for reform realised in ways he never would have imagined or intended.

When the Vichy government was established, steps were taken to form industrial organisations to regulate all aspects of the economy, and in that context COIC was established. COIC was officially recognised on 2 November 1940. As Evelyn Ehrlich describes it, COIC brought together the film industry's desire to maintain French production with the Vichy government's desire to impose corporate structures on all industries. Although Guy de Carmoy, who became Vichy's head of the cinema division in August, was not in favour of collaboration, he feared that if the French did not control the French film industry, the Germans would. Like many if not most members of the film industry, Carmoy saw the survival of French cinema threatened by Continental.[14]

Hence COIC was often at odds with Continental. Yet the first activities of COIC – activities meant to protect and nourish the French film industry – were not only reflective of the Nazi practices of anti-Semitism, but went further than what was expected or required. The first anti-Semitic laws enacted in France prohibited Jews from being heads of companies; by issuing obligatory professional cards to all film personnel, which required proof of Aryan identity, COIC was effectively banning all Jews from all work in the industry. As Jean-Pierre Bertin-Maghit puts it: 'Contrary to what happened in other professions, the application of statutes concerning Jews in the cinema went beyond what was required by law, which concerned only heads of business and department heads. Here, the law applied to everyone [i.e., all Jews who worked in the cinema]. This zealous excess was undoubtedly the result of xenophobic movements that were widespread throughout the 1930s.'[15]

The pages of the earliest issues of *Le Film* demonstrate the price paid by COIC for the safeguarding of the film industry. In 1940 and 1941, German films were shown widely in France, and *Le Film* praised the films and their stars, like Zarah Leander and Ilse Werner. Particular praise was accorded the anti-Semitic propaganda film *Jew Süss*. The film was discussed in several issues of the journal, where it is referred to as a 'brilliant work'.[16] A commentary on *Les Tribus du cinéma et du théâtre*, Lucien Rebatet's hateful diatribe against supposed Jewish influence in the theatre and the cinema, notes that the 'violence' of Rebatet's work is completely necessary. The author writes: 'Those of us in the cinema have been damaged by twenty years of cohabitation with Jews, who for the most part are foreigners just out of the ghetto. […] Getting rid of these unsavoury individuals is the responsibility of our directors. Rediscovering the correct way to proceed is our job, those of us in the industry.'[17] There is a disturbing tendency in some accounts of cinema during the Second World War to praise COIC for saving the industry, while attributing the dreadful practices of the organisation to Vichy alone. Jacques Siclier, for instance, does not shy away from acknowledging the practices of COIC insofar as anti-Semitic legislation is concerned, but, by treating anti-Semitism and the regulation of the French film industry as two different elements, a far more disturbing question is avoided – whether, in the hearts and minds of those who were devoted to the survival of French cinema, ridding the industry of Jews was not only desirable, but essential to that survival.[18]

Much has been made of the fact that at Continental, Greven knowingly hired a Jewish screenwriter, Jean-Paul Le Chanois (whose given name was Jean-Paul Dreyfus). Producer and director Roger Richebé tells how, in 1942, Greven told him that the best cinema personnel were Jews. Naturally not quite knowing how to respond, Richebé said nothing until Greven, clearly referring to Le Chanois, confided in him: 'I have a Jew working for me, but he doesn't know that I know…'[19] In other words, while COIC was enthusiastically purging the film industry of any possible Jewish 'contamination', Greven was making exceptions that never would have got through the required bureaucratic steps imposed by COIC for employment in the industry. Yet the fact that Greven was willing to look the other way insofar as Le Chanois was concerned suggests only that he was an opportunist as far as Nazi law was concerned. Greven was not above threatening retaliation against Jewish loved ones in order to get what he wanted; according to actress Edwige Feuillère, Greven forced her to make *Mam'zelle Bonaparte* (directed by Maurice Tourneur, 1942) by threatening her Jewish friend and companion with deportation.[20]

Throughout the period of the Occupation, COIC and Continental clashed in different ways, and in virtually every case, the central issue was whether the French would retain control over the industry. Since Continental was officially a French company, any protests by COIC about German interference were handily dismissed. In a confidential report about the activities of COIC, dated 17 July 1941, what was never stated in the pages of *Le Film* is stated clearly: 'Continental Films competes with and handicaps French production. By hiring, since November 1940, the best French directors, artists, and technicians, Continental Films wants to limit the output of French productions.'[21] The unfair advantage held by Continental, and the somewhat naïve belief that because Continental was officially a French company, it would be accountable to the same rules as any other French film organisation, led COIC to take a number of positions (sometimes clandestinely) to preserve its turf.

Consider, for example, one of COIC's complaints about Continental concerning the status of the film director. The well-known directors who had made French films during the 1930s, like Christian-Jaque and Henri Decoin, and who worked for Continental, gave the company an appearance of both historical continuity and French integrity. While many of the directors at Continental had already-established careers, Continental also gave some men their first opportunity to direct, among them Clouzot, André Cayatte and the actor Fernandel. The practice was common at other studios as well, and film-makers Jacques Becker and Robert Bresson made their feature film debuts during the war. In April 1942, film-maker and COIC official Louis Daquin outlined what was seen as a dangerous situation: 'For some time we've seen well-known writers and actors announce their intentions to direct films that they have either written or star in.'[22] Aside from Clouzot, Cayatte and Fernandel, other names included in the list include Jean Anouilh and J.P. Feydeau for the writers, and René Dary and Pierry Fresnay among the actors. Daquin called the practice a threat to those who were 'professional directors', particularly since writers and actors already has a job.[23] Despite Daquin's implication that these writers and actors were taking jobs away from those in need, many film personnel did indeed leave the country, whether by choice or necessity, and there were many opportunities created for first-time directors. Continental is not named specifically by Daquin, but since most of the names he mentions were affiliated with the firm, it seems likely that this was an example of the fear of Continental's authority – not only the authority to produce French films, but to violate established notions of film authorship. This concern about authorship seems like a bureaucratic obsession to award credentials to the right people, but it is also an attempt to challenge the right of the German occupiers to create flexibility in the professional ranks of the cinema. That Clouzot was one of the beneficiaries of this flexibility contributed to his controversial status.

Immediately after the defeat of France, film-making in the occupied zone was prohibited by the Occupation forces, and Continental cemented its authority by producing films that provided a welcome change from the German films that were promoted in France.[24] Continental's first six films were released in France between August and October 1941. *Premier rendez-vous/First Rendez-Vous* (directed by Henri Decoin and starring Danielle Darrieux), a romantic comedy, was the first Continental film released in France, on 14 August. *Le Dernier des six/Last of the Six* followed (released 16 September). The remaining Continental films of the year were *Le Club des soupirants/Nine Bachelors* (directed by Maurice Gleize, 26 September), *L'Assassinat du Père Noël/The Assassination of Father Christmas* (directed by Christian-Jaque, 16 October), *Ne bougez plus/Stay Still* (directed by Pierre Caron, 31 October) and *Péchés de jeunesse/Sins of Youth* (directed by Maurice Tourneur, 16 November). With the exception of *L'Assassinat du Père Noël* and *Le Dernier des six*, all of Continental's first group of films were variations on the genre of romantic comedy, thus suggesting that Continental's primary role would be to make films that would distract the public. *L'Assassinat du Père Noël* and *Le Dernier des six* were different, for they were mystery films with a twist – the fantastic, in the case of the former, and dark comedy, in the case of the latter.

It is common to refer to the films made by Continental – as well as most of the films made during the Occupation – as 'diversions'. While it requires little imagination to grasp that film audiences would indeed seek in movie theatres some kind of 'escape' from the realities of war and Occupation, too often the very term 'diversion' is used to obscure the possibility that distraction and entertainment can reveal important understandings of how the Occupation was lived, understood and experienced by the French. As a blanket term, 'distraction' does little to clarify what contributed to the success of Continental's films. The films produced by Continental were mysteries, comedies and dramas; some were light in tone, while others were dark and ominous. There were adaptations, some of nineteenth-century works of French literature (André Cayatte's adaptation of Zola's novel *Au bonheur des dames/The Ladies' Paradise*, 1943, and of Maupassant's novel *Pierre et Jean*, 1943), others of works by mystery novelist Georges Simenon (who was the most often adapted author of the Occupation and who in 1942 signed a contract with Continental), including *Annette et la dame blonde/Annette and the Blonde Woman* (Jean Dréville, 1942) and *Picpus* (Richard Pottier, 1943). Continental's films featured the most popular actors of the day, from Danielle Darrieux and Ginette Leclerc to Albert Préjean and Pierre Fresnay, and the stars of Continental films were featured regularly in fan magazines like *Ciné-mondial* and *Vedettes*. Some of Continental's films seemed to function – despite Greven's assurances that there would be no propaganda expected of film-makers – as not so subtle reminders of the decadence of the pre-war period (Raimu's famous speech denouncing the bourgeoisie in *Les Inconnus dans la maison/Strangers in the House* (1942), discussed in more detail below), or of the promises of a 'new order' unifying Europe (Mouret's speech at the conclusion of *Au bonheur des dames* announces a new era of 'collaboration' [specifically between the workers and management of the department store], which would have been difficult *not* to see equally as the promise of French–German collaboration).

One of the questions most commonly raised about *Le Corbeau* has to do with how and why a film that seems to reflect so directly upon the common wartime practice of anonymous letter-writing could have been made by a Nazi organisation. Thus it is important to consider how the practice of censorship worked vis-à-vis films made for Continental. One of the many ironies of the Occupation, of course, is that directors at Continental did not have to go through the censorship channels otherwise imposed on French directors. French film-makers who worked there had far more liberty than they would have had they worked at any other production company during the war. This does not mean that any and all film subjects would be allowed at Continental, yet several Continental films are surprising for how much they suggest the possibility of a critical view of collaboration. Indeed, Evelyn Ehrlich states: 'A few filmmakers working at Continental took advantage of the relative freedom from censorship constraints ... to insert veiled messages of nationalism and even resistance in their films.' Had Continental been concerned with censoring its films, says Ehrlich, three would have made them particularly uncomfortable.[25]

The first is Christian-Jaques's 1941 film *L'Assassinat du Père Noël*, which ends (in a sharp detour from the novel by Pierre Véry from which it was adapted) with a declaration of French pride in the face of adversity. Harry Baur, who plays the role of a globemaker, tells a child at the film's end of a beautiful French princess who is asleep: 'One might have thought she was dead,' says Baur's character. 'And there are those who would have thought so, but they are wrong. She was very much alive and in her sleep she had a dream, a marvelous dream, always the same one. She dreamt of a Prince Charming who would one day come and awaken her and bring her happiness.' Ehrlich reads the statement as 'hope of eventual liberation', and suggests that Continental was 'unaware of its thinly veiled allusion to De Gaulle and the Free French ...'.[26] The second 'uncomfortable' film was *La Symphonie fantastique* (1942, also by Christian-Jaque), the story of Hector Berlioz. In telling a tale of the famous musician the film also tells a tale of national pride (the film was indeed censored, but even the final version can be seen as exceeding the boundaries of permissible representations of loyalty to France). Finally, Maurice Tourneur's *La Main du diable* (1943) takes the tale of a Faustian bargain – a topic one might well imagine to be taboo in an occupied country – and opposes sacrifice for the better good to self-interest and greed (that the film was written by Jewish screenwriter Jean Paul Le Chanois, who was a member of both the Communist Party and the Resistance, adds even more levels of complexity to the film).

If the notion of 'diversion' is limited in usefulness, one must also be wary of reading Continental films as informed by a spirit of resistance.[27] The conclusion of *L'Assassinat du Père Noël* is ambiguous enough to suggest that France is awaiting the formation of the 'new Europe' as much as the arrival of Resistance forces. While ambiguity may well be a form of resistance to the occupier, too much emphasis on ambiguity as exceptional takes attention away from the complex ways in which most Occupation films engaged, in however muted or displaced ways, with the contemporary situation. *Le Corbeau* can be read as an indictment of a culture where surveillance and betrayal are everyday practices. And if we are to believe Clouzot's own account, the film effectively ended his career because of its dangerous subject matter. But given critical elements in other Continental films, like those described above, it might well be more productive to consider these examples not as subversive hidden messages, but as demonstrations of the role played by the cinema in the practice of collaboration. In other words, the apparent freedom of expression given to artists in the employ of Continental created the impression that at least in the realm of the cinema, the Nazis were amenable to fictions that gave audiences the impression that in the movie theatres, imaginary reconstructions of the very nature of the Occupation were permissible. *Le Corbeau* may well be an exceptional film in this regard. But it was not the only Continental film to suggest that German control of the French film industry was far more flexible, insofar as individual films were concerned, than the typical practice of German censorship would suggest.[28]

In the four years of the Occupation, the cinema was a site of contestation and negotiation. To be sure, France was controlled by Germany, and Continental's power was close to absolute. Yet the very nature of German censorship in the film industry, which was quite different from any other media organisation during the war, needs to be understood as a process that not only 'allowed' a range of topics with various implications, but encouraged them, as long as certain topics – overt French nationalism, or anything that could suggest a positive view of England – were not broached. German censorship was of course brutal during the Second World War, but Continental constituted a particular and peculiar case. Rather than assume that French film-makers were able to 'slip in' various subtexts or Resistance-inspired nods to French audiences, it is more likely that the German censors – including Alfred Greven – missed nothing, and instead saw Continental as producing the positive face of French–German collaboration. In other words, broad freedom of expression and topics promoted the idea that German domination was good for France.

Even though directors at Continental had access to materials, equipment and resources unlike those of any other company during the war, circumstances changed in the course of the Occupation. First, the very nature of the war changed. During the first two years of the Occupation, it was a commonly held belief that the Germans would indeed succeed in establishing Nazi rule in Europe.[29] In 1943, and particularly at mid-year, however, when German attention focused more on the Eastern Front and less on the inevitable victory of the Reich, the end of German Occupation was in sight. Second, the goals and visions of Continental Films changed. Initially, with the establishment of the company and the hiring of French personnel, Greven sought to create a cinema that would be emblematic of French–German collaboration in the New Europe. But that notion of the cinema, and of collaboration, did not endure. Twenty Continental films had their premieres before the end of the summer of 1943, and most of the rest of the films shown in 1943 had begun production earlier in the year. The resources once available for Continental were diverted to military ends. When Le Corbeau premiered in September 1943, the end of the war was in sight. We will of course never know if the film would have been as controversial as it was had it been made in 1941 or 1942, or whether Clouzot himself would have been in a position to make such a film earlier on in his career at Continental; in any case, the fate of Le Corbeau as a controversial film is very much a function of its timing.

It is well known that cinemas were crowded during the Occupation.[30] The common-sense view of the popularity of cinema is that the theatres were warm and that films were – once again – a 'diversion' from the Occupation. There is no doubt that cinemas were warm spaces, but so were (some) cafés, theatres and other venues for popular entertainment. Just as the term 'diversion' can function as a convenient catch-all to discourage any serious analysis of individual films, it can also be a way to suggest that the cinema is not a 'serious' matter in a time of war. It is more productive to take 'diversion' seriously, and to ask what was specific to the appeal of cinema to French citizens during the war. If it is common to use the term 'diversion' to describe the popularity of the cinema during periods of tumult and crisis, 'diversion' is better described in terms of the imaginary worlds the cinema created not only as a defence against the world outside but as an engagement with that world. Screenwriter Jean Aurenche said of filmgoing during the Occupation: 'Filmgoing for the French was a fabulous evasion. Films allowed the French to forget, together – in spaces where they could at last get warm – the difficulties of everyday life, fear, and sadness.'[31] The cinema functioned as a public space, where the threat of surveillance, so evident everywhere in French public life, could be momentarily dispelled, even if very precariously (houselights were kept on during the projection of newsreels, to discourage people from booing them; lines outside of the cinema became, later in the war, recruiting sites for the STO (Service de Travail Obligatoire, obligatory work detail in Germany). There was no such thing as a completely safe space during the war, but the cinema provided the opportunity for French citizens to experience, collectively, a sense of escape *and* engagement simultaneously.

One of the most striking aspects of the films made during the Occupation is how taken up they are with questions of gender. Crises of male authority abound in films of the period, frequently accompanied by an attendant preoccupation with women's status. The cinema may well be a technology and a form so structured by the gendered polarity of the look that it is always attentive to gender, but every embodiment of that polarity is shaped by specific historical conditions. In the world of Occupation cinema, male authority is undermined in one way or another, from the alcoholic lawyer unable to leave his home, in *Les Inconnus dans la maison,* to the artist unable to satisfy his desires (and, perhaps more importantly, those of his female companion) until he makes a bargain with the devil in *La Main du diable.* Women's authority takes on surprising contours; in *Premier rendez-vous,* for instance, Danielle Darrieux confronts a classroom full of young men about their mocking treatment of their teacher, played by Fernand Ledoux, in a scene quite evocative of the famous scene in Dorothy Arzner's *Dance, Girl, Dance* (1940) when Judy confronts her mostly male audience about how she sees them. *Marie-Martine* (Albert Valentin, 1943) is a retelling of what many consider the quintessential poetic realist film of the 1930s, Carné's *Le Jour se lève*, but from a woman's point of view, and here, as in other films of the era, women's narrative authority consistently undermines that of men.

Noël Burch and Geneviève Sellier's study of gender in French cinema over a 25-year period regards Occupation cinema as representing a major shift from the male-centred dramas of the 1930s. In their view, Occupation cinema consistently displayed patriarchal power in crisis, with attendant representations of men who are decidedly not icons of traditional masculinity and women who have far more power and authority than had previously been the case in French film. Recalling Jean Guéhenno's description of Pétain's announcement of the armistice on the radio (an 'old man who speaks in the voice of an old woman'), they attribute part of the inspiration for this stunning change in French film to the image of Pétain as a weak old man who embodies all too well the defeat of France.[32] The fear of emasculation, of a feminised France passively acquiescing to German authority, permeated France, and it is perhaps in the cinema where these anxieties found their most heightened and influential expressions. If going to the cinema was indeed a diversion for French audiences, the diversion didn't necessarily take them away from key issues of the era, but rather allowed them to engage with them in imaginative ways.

Henri-Georges Clouzot

How, then, did Henri-Georges Clouzot arrive at his exceptional position at Continental films? Born in 1907 in Niort, a small city in the central west area of France, Clouzot shared a love of theatre and cinema with his siblings, but only later in his life did the possibility of a career in stage or screen become a possibility. Clouzot went to Naval School and studied international law and political science, hoping for a career in the diplomatic corps. But, through a series of fortuitous encounters, Clouzot began writing for the cinema. His first credited work occurred in 1931, when he worked on the screenplays for *Le Chanteur inconnu, Je serai seule après minuit, Ma cousine de Varsovie, Le Roi des palaces* and *Un Soir de rafle*. Virtually all of the work that Clouzot did in film in the early 1930s was in Germany.[33] In 1934, Clouzot returned to France (according to him, he was forced to leave because he was too friendly with one of his producers, who was Jewish).[34] In Paris he met the renowned actor Louis Jouvet, who encouraged Clouzot's theatrical work (Jouvet left France during the Second World War; he would eventually star in Clouzot's first post-war film, *Quai des Orfèvres*). Clouzot's career was taking off when he was diagnosed with tuberculosis and was forced to spend four years in sanatoriums. Clouzot, then, left Germany shortly after the ascendancy of the Third Reich in 1933. Many of his compatriots, some of whom would eventually work at Continental, continued to make films in Germany throughout most of the 1930s.

When Clouzot returned to Paris in 1938, he immediately began working on film screenplays. He made the acquaintance of two individuals who would be important figures during the next several years of his life. He met Suzy Delair when he was casting a film. The two became companions and collaborated successfully on two films for Continental (*Le Dernier des six* and *L'Assassin habite au 21*). Their relationship lasted 12 years. Clouzot met the actor Pierre Fresnay, who was about to direct his first film, *Le Duel* (1939). Clouzot was hired to adapt the screenplay. The film – the one and only film directed by Fresnay – did not do well, but the two men forged a friendship (Clouzot later said that Pierre Fresnay helped him more than anyone else during his lifetime).[35] Fresnay starred in both of the films that Clouzot directed for Continental (*L'Assassin habite au 21* and *Le Corbeau*).

Clouzot's health problems kept him from military service. He continued to work in the theatre (his play *On prend les mêmes* opened on 4 December 1940 in Paris). Greven knew Clouzot from Berlin, and soon Clouzot was hired by Continental to adapt a novel by Stanislas-André Steeman to the screen. This was *Le Dernier des six*, directed by Georges Lacombe. The film starred Pierre Fresnay, his first Occupation film and one of several he would star in for Continental. For Clouzot, the film was the first of three that he would adapt by the Belgian author, who was never pleased with the radical changes that Clouzot brought to his works. Steeman's 1930 mystery novel *Six hommes morts* (*Six Dead Men*) (later retitled, after the film, *Le Dernier des six*) concerns a group of six male friends who make a pact to separate and to pursue their fortunes individually, and then to meet in five years to share their bounty. The novel opens as two of the men, Senterre and Perlonjour, await the arrival of their four allies. Waiting with them is the fiancée (Asuncion) of one of the six men (Gernicot); she has not seen Gernicot for two years. News arrives that one of the awaited men has died under somewhat suspicious circumstances just before the arrival of the ship on which he was sailing. One by one, the other members of the group die, until only Senterre and Perlonjour are left. Both men have fallen in love with Asuncion, and after the apparent death of Gernicot shortly after his arrival, their attentions to her intensify.

The inspector on the case is Wens, Steeman's best-known creation, who is featured in a number of the author's mysteries. Wens, short for Wenceslas Vorobeïtchik, is a dapper and sometimes acerbic investigator. He handily solves the case, but not without many complications – especially the fact that almost all of the men are murdered before the solution is made apparent. Gernicot was the murderer of the first victim, and, with the help of an accomplice, he staged his own death (and later substituted the accomplice's mutilated body for his own) and proceeded to kill the remaining members of the group. Only Perlonjour is spared, thanks to Wens's realisation that the murderer is one of the six men. The rationale for the murders was money, but Gernicot was motivated as well by jealousy, for he was aware of the attentions aroused by Asuncion – revealed to be his wife, not his fiancée – and attempted his final murder (of Senterre) in a state of jealous rage.

The basic premise of the novel is maintained in the film, but Clouzot's screenplay also adds two significant and interrelated threads. First, he adds a theatrical dimension nowhere present in the novel. While in the novel few details are given as to how the men made (or did not make) their fortunes, Senterre in the film has made his fortune in the world of music halls and spectacles. His profession becomes the premise for the introduction of several theatrical performances in the film. The character of Asuncion (now named Lolita, played by Michèle Alfa), who accompanies Gernicot to the scene of his murder, is a performer, 'la reine de la cible' ('queen of sharpshooting'), as the promotional fan she gives Senterre illustrates. She performed in Dakar, where she met Gernicot, and she asks Senterre to feature her on stage to help her financially. A fair amount of screen time is devoted to Lolita's appearance on stage as a sharpshooter who takes aim at balloons held by women on stage.

Second, the 'theatrics' added by Clouzot to the mystery plot are enhanced by what is undoubtedly Clouzot's most noteworthy addition to Steeman's novel, the female character Mila Malou. Mila is an aspiring singer and the girlfriend of Wens (thus creating a very different kind of detective; in the novel he is single and is described as misogynist). Suzy Delair, herself a successful stage performer, plays the role of Mila, and her performance of the flighty, high-strung Mila is over the top, as befits her character. Mila wears somewhat gaudy clothing and shrieks rather than speaks at a breakneck speed. In contrast to the reticence of most of the characters in the film, she talks with virtually no sense of restraint. Mila provides comic relief in the film, and she is thus central to the creation of the kind of hybrid mystery/comedy that turned out to be popular during the Occupation.

On the basis of his success in the adaptation of Steeman's novel – and undoubtedly his connections with Pierre Fresnay and his successful introduction of Suzy Delair to the screen didn't hurt – Clouzot was hired as the head of the screenplay division at Continental. He wrote another screenplay in 1941, an adaptation of *Les Inconnus dans la maison*, a novel by Georges Simenon. The film was directed by Henri Decoin and starred Raimu in the role of Loursat, an alcoholic lawyer who has withdrawn from the world since his wife left him and his daughter many years before. Pierre Fresnay provided the voiceover in the film, which emphasised Simenon's tone of darkness and foreboding. When a dead body is discovered in the house that Loursat and his daughter Nicole share, he learns that Nicole has been part of a gang of teenagers (all the other members are male) who hang out at a local bar and who perform various pranks and initiation rites, of which the dead man is one casualty. Loursat agrees to defend Nicole's boyfriend, Manu, when he is accused of the man's murder.

In Simenon's novel, the guilty party is Luska, who is in love with Nicole, and his Jewish identity is presented in vile anti-Semitic terms. Interestingly, the explicit anti-Semitism of the novel is not present in the same way in the film, although the casting of Mouloudji, a French-Algerian singer and actor, in the role of Luska could easily be said to suggest racial stereotypes of the criminal. If the anti-Semitism of the novel is not presented so explicitly in the film, Clouzot made an addition to the film that has become its most famous – and notorious – aspect. The scene, not present in the novel, occurs during Loursat's courtroom defence of Manu. Quiet during most of the proceedings, Loursat, in Raimu's inimitably dramatic style, suddenly holds forth about the town's lack of values, about parents' lack of commitment to their children, about the number of bars and brothels:

> Gentlemen of the jury, can you show me the way to the stadium, the velodrome, the swimming pool? No, don't try, there is no stadium, velodrome, or pool. There are 132 cafés and bistros, I counted them, and 4 bordellos – those, I didn't count. My fellow citizens marked the path to them long ago. Gentlemen, when children cannot get drunk on fresh air and activity, they must seek recreation somewhere. They go to the movies and are spellbound by gangsters, when they are not aroused by the legs of the vamp. And one fine night these spectators, these children, become the actors, and they cover themselves with blood. And this mantle of blood – it is you, it is we – who have thrown it over their shoulders.[36]

The scene is generally understood as a Vichy-values speech. By and large, however, Continental films tended not to follow the same quest for morality and uplift as did explicitly Vichy films. It's tempting to 'excuse' the scene by suggesting, for example, that the speech was written more to give Raimu the possibility of holding forth than to promote a moral agenda. And the anti-bourgeois politics of the scene could have appeared in another film of another time without suggesting a fascist agenda. But of course this wasn't another time, and Clouzot's screenplay, at least at the particular moment of the dramatic discourse, comes quite close to the propaganda that Continental was presumably so determined to avoid.[37]

Clouzot directed his first film for Continental in 1942. Like *Le Dernier des six*, *L'Assassin habite au 21* was an adaptation of a mystery novel by Steeman, and like the previous film, it evoked the anger of Steeman, who protested about all of Clouzot's adaptations that the director needed to 'destroy' in order to create.[38] As in the earlier film, Clouzot partners detective Wens with Mila Malou, played once again by Fresnay and Delair. The setting of the film is moved from London to Paris (one clear taboo for Continental personnel was any mention of England that could be construed as favourable), and Wens is on the track of a serial killer who leaves his calling card, inscribed with the name 'Monsieur Durand', at the scene of every crime. Once again, Clouzot expands the film to include not only the mystery but also Mila Malou's show-business career (matching Suzy Delair's own off-screen singing career). Early in the film, Mila is trying to sell herself as a singer to an impresario, and he tells her that she needs to have a recognisable name, and to illustrate his point he grabs a newspaper and points to the story about the serial killer. Mila thus becomes as committed in her own way as Wens to solving the mystery, assuming that the fame she will acquire will assure her success on stage.

Wens receives a tip that the killer is a resident of a pension at 21, rue Junot. He poses as a pastor and moves into the house, populated by an odd assortment of eccentrics, including Mlle Cuq (who describes herself as a 'vraie jeune fille'), a writer who cannot get a manuscript accepted; a blind boxer, Kid Robert; a magician, Lalah-Poor; Linz, a former colonial officer; and Colin, who fabricates faceless dolls made to resemble what is known of the serial killer (i.e., nothing). Mila Malou quickly discovers that Wens is hot on the trail of the killer, so she too moves into the boarding house. The killings continue, and one seemingly false suspect is arrested after another. Almost at the same moment, Wens and Mila realise, separately, that the three men who have been arrested (Lalah-Poor, Linz and Colin), and then let go when another murder was committed during their jail time, are working in concert; Monsieur Durand is three men, not one. Wens is taken at gunpoint from the house once the killers realise he is on to them. Meanwhile, Mila, who has several opportunities to perform in the course of the film, begins to see multiples of '3' everywhere she looks as she sings for the assembled guests at the boarding house. She takes the police to the place where the three men are holding Wens. Hence the crime is solved, and Wens and Malou are presumably happily reunited.

L'Assassin habite au 21 continues the hybrid genre of mystery and comedy initiated by *Le Dernier des six*. While Clouzot is best remembered for *Le Corbeau*, he was arguably the individual most responsible for the immediate success of the comedy/mystery format that became popular during the Occupation. Mila Malou is as brassy, energetic and somewhat hysterical as she was in the earlier film, and her dialogue is witty and over the top. The film is as much about her and Wens's relationship as it is about the solving of the crime, and that relationship has verbal sparring at its core. In some ways their repartee is reminiscent of American screwball comedies of the 1930s, like *Bringing Up Baby* and *His Girl Friday*. The comparison is not as far-fetched as it might seem initially. Since American films were banned in France during the Occupation, French directors could move into territories previously dominated by Hollywood films. And Greven was eager for French cinema to provide competition for American films in the 'new Europe'.

Although *L'Assassin habite au 21* does not receive sustained treatment in Burch and Sellier's analysis of the cinema during the Occupation, Clouzot's first film as a director reveals many of the preoccupations that made films of the period so interesting for their representations of gender.[39] Mila Malou may well be a stereotype of femininity, easily read in 'either/or' terms – either a stereotype of the ditzy female, or a stereotype so excessive that it (rather than she) is mocked. She is, nonetheless, an integral part of the intrigue of the film, and she and Wens solve the mystery separately, each on her/his own terms. The figure of Mlle Cuq, the unsuccessful mystery writer, is strongly suggestive of the kind of narrative authority often associated with women in Occupation cinema. She is murdered by 'Monsieur Durand' when she comes up with the idea to write a mystery about the boarding house itself, that is, when she comes dangerously close to uncovering the men's secret before the detective or his companion do.

There is also a strong element of what could be called, for lack of a better term, 'earthiness' (or vulgarity) in the film, and most often the one who embodies it is Mila Malou, whether in her enthusiastic popping of blackheads on Wens's forehead, or in her somewhat peculiar, and always energetic, turns of phrase. For instance, early in the film, during our first introduction to Mila Malou, the character is attempting to spark the interest of an impresario. She says: 'You're like the gardener who cultivates fragile little plants, like the little pile of manure that keeps the young shoots warm, and I'm the plant climbing upwards, toward the sky...I need a tutor, in other words, I'm like America before Christopher Columbus.'

This film is also set in the 'contemporain vague' of Occupation cinema, with one reference to 1930s French cinema (the name of the boarding house is 'Pension Mimosas', the title of a well-known 1935 film by Jacques Feyder) and another that contradicts the 'vague present tense' assumed to be characteristic of Occupation cinema.

At the conclusion of *L'Assassin habite au 21*, the three murderers are caught as Mila Malou and the police come to the rescue of Wens. The three men are ordered to put up their hands, and the final image of the film shows Wens as he lowers the right arm of Lalah-Poor in order to light a match behind the murderer's ear. Thus Lalah-Poor is standing, immobile, with his left arm extended in the air – performing the Nazi salute. There is an element of mockery in this moment, but one could hardly refer to this image in any kind of subversive way; rather it seems to indicate precisely the tone of dark humour that is so characteristic of Clouzot's style. After the Liberation, one of the pieces of evidence brought against Clouzot was that he was seen making the Nazi one-armed salute, and one cannot help but wonder if the last image of the film was confused with the director himself.

Given the popularity of the Delair–Fresnay duo in *Le Dernier des six*, it is not surprising that *L'Assassin habite au 21* was a critical and popular success. A reviewer for *Le Miroir de l'Ecran* noted the delighted responses of viewers at the premiere of the film, in particular at how 'amusing and witty scenes alternate judiciously with more severe and dramatic ones', thus creating a 'clever cocktail of humor and drama'.[40] Clouzot's directorial debut was praised as well. The reviewer for the collaborationist fan magazine *Ciné-mondial* noted that the director had a large role to play in the success of the film. 'H.-G. Clouzot, neo-director, but also a screenwriter who knows his work, has put the finishing touches on a production that is dense, concise, mobile, varied, all in the service of a rich imagination.'[41] Thus Clouzot's directorial career was launched. Clouzot was focused on his film career, but he also continued his interests in the theatre. Before the premiere of *L'Assassin habite au 21* on 8 July 1942, Clouzot's play *Comédie en trois actes*, written for his friends Pierre Fresnay and Fresnay's wife Yvonne Printemps, opened in March of that year.

Clouzot may have worked consistently with a group of actors who admired and respected him, but *L'Assassin habite au 21* also made evident Clouzot's reputation as a demanding, sometimes violent, director. Suzy Delair describes how Clouzot was able to get the results he wanted: 'Clouzot slapped me. So what? He slapped others as well. He could only get the best out of his actors by hitting them … He was tough, but I'm not about to complain.'[42] 'He worked relentlessly, which made for a juicy spectacle,' declared Pierre Fresnay in describing the director. 'That's to say nothing of his taste for violence, which he never tried with me …'[43] In February of 1943, Clouzot began to work on *Le Corbeau*, and the actors' accounts describe a director who was brilliant and demanding, but who once again was physically abusive, and who created an atmosphere of dread on the set.[44]

One can see traces of his previous work in this film, but the lighthearted (if always a bit vulgar) comedy has virtually disappeared. Gone is the witty repartee between Suzy Delair and Pierre Fresnay, as if to suggest that the comedy/mystery genre was for Clouzot a stepping stone to a film that exemplifies film noir with its use of light and dark contrast and shadowy atmospheres, and its characters caught up in webs of deception. The project began when Clouzot read the initial script by Louis Chavance, who had written several scripts for Occupation films (although *Le Corbeau*, the final version co-authored with Clouzot, was the only film he made for Continental), including Marcel L'Herbier's *La Nuit fantastique* (1942) and Jacques Becker's *Le Dernier atout* (1942). According to Clouzot, no one at Continental was enthused by the project. Bauermeister (in charge of production) thought the subject was too 'violent and hard' and Greven deemed the film 'extremely dangerous'. Yet Clouzot wanted to make what he called this 'revolutionary' film, and Greven reluctantly told him to go ahead with it.[45] As we shall see in part 2, the preparation of the script of *Le Corbeau* involved a complex process of revision with screenwriter Louis Chavance, and the evolution of the script is enormously interesting in terms of assumptions about crime, gender and retribution.

When Clouzot directed *L'Assassin habite au 21*, the budget was generous, and included materials that seemed extravagant by pre-war standards.[46] While it is true that Continental always had access to materials that were otherwise restricted, things changed drastically during the war, and, by the time of the production of *Le Corbeau*, restrictions on electricity meant that films had to be shot at night, and actors worked on sets with little or no heat. The filming of *Le Corbeau* took place in Montfort-L'Amaury, a small town west of Paris.

The cast and crew went there by train, in the freezing cold, and often under the threat of air attacks.

Any serious examination of French cinema of the Occupation raises a number of perplexing questions concerning our assumptions about the nature of collaboration and censorship. The most obvious answer to the question – how and why did the German Occupation of France 'save' French cinema? – seems at best insulting (the French were weak; the Germans took charge) and at worst an apology for the cinematic equivalent of making the trains run on time. As we have seen, the development of Continental films allowed the flourishing of French cinema for a variety of reasons, ranging from Greven's own love of the cinema to the need to address the crises that affected French film in the 1930s, from the possibilities created for French artists through the absence of competition to the material possibilities provided by Continental.

Le Corbeau is both typical and exceptional in its relationship to French Occupation cinema. It is 'typical' in the sense that it benefited from all of the factors that made Continental successful. But it is also exceptional for many reasons. It brings together some of the best features of Occupation film-making – the development of a film noir style, the thematisation of surveillance, the complexities of film narration in relationship to questions of gender and sexuality. If the film succeeds on its own terms, it is also exceptional in that it has come to stand so emblematically for the period of the German Occupation of France.

Notes

1   The most influential account of this change in how the period is understood is Paxton, Robert, *Vichy France: Old Guard and New Order, 1940–1944* (New York: Columbia University Press, 1972). See also Jackson, Julian, *France: The Dark Years, 1940–1944* (Oxford and New York: Oxford University Press, 2001).

2   Ehrlich: *Cinema of Paradox: French Filmmaking Under the German Occupation*, p. x.

3   For a list and description of all of the films made during the war, see Siclier, Jacques, *La France de Pétain et son cinéma* (Paris: Editions Henri Veyrier, 1981), pp. 257–436.

4   Siclier: *La France de Pétain et son cinéma*, pp. 15–24.

5   Bessy, Maurice, in Maurice Bessy and Raymond Chirat, *Histoire du cinéma français: Encyclopédie des films, 1940–1950* (Paris: Pygmalion/Gérard Watelet, 1991), p. 15.

6   Different interpretations have been offered concerning the relationship between Greven and Goebbels, particularly insofar as their differing understandings of what kinds of films Continental should make. Goebbels's famous remark, that 'only light, frothy and, if possible corny pictures are desired' (cited in Ehrlich: *Cinema of Paradox: French Filmmaking Under the German Occupation*, p. 141), has been read as indicative of a profound difference of opinion between the two men, but Goebbels's remarks have also been understood as insignificant in relationship to the French film industry. See Bertin-Maghit, Jean-Pierre, *Le Cinéma français sous l'Occupation* (Paris: Perrin, 1989; rpt. 2002), pp. 22–23; Crisp, Colin, *The Classic French Cinema* (Bloomington: Indiana University Press, 1993; rpt. 1997), pp. 48–49; Ehrlich: *Cinema of Paradox: French Filmmaking Under the German Occupation*, pp. 135–157.

7   Chateau, René, *Le Cinéma français sous l'Occupation, 1940–1944* (Paris: Editions René Chateau, 1996), pp. 11, 13.

8   Pithon, Rémy, 'Cinéma français et cinéma allemand des années trente: de l'échange à l'exil', in *Entre Locarno et Vichy: Les Relations culturelles franco-allemandes dans les années 1930*, edited by Hans Manfred Bock, Reinhart Meyer-Kalkus and Michel Trebitsch (Paris: CNRS Editions, 1993), p. 595.

9   Darrieux, Danielle, with Jean-Pierre Ferrière, *Danielle Darrieux: Filmographie commentée par elle-même* (Paris: Editions Ramsay Cinema, 1995), pp. 55–56. See also Bertin-Maghit: *Le Cinéma français sous l'Occupation*, p. 167.

10   NA, 'Une société de production s'est créé: "Continental Films"', *Le Film* 2 (1 November 1940), p. 12.

11   According to Carné, Greven assured him that other directors had signed on (which they hadn't yet done), and told other directors that Carné had signed on before he had signed a contract. See Carné, Marcel, with Claude Guiget, *La Vie à belles dents: Souvenirs* (Paris: J.-P. Ollivier, 1975), pp. 177–180.

12   Susan Hayward suggests that the establishment of COIC during the Occupation reflects a general tendency in French history: 'Peculiar to the political culture of France is the fact that, ever since the birth of France as a Republic, it is rather in her moments of anti-republicanism that she appears to facilitate order, Bonapartism being the first example. On a small scale we can see this in the establishing of the COIC during the Occupation.' See *French National Cinema* (London and New York: Routledge, 1993), p. 125.

13   Bertin-Maghit: *Le Cinéma français sous l'Occupation*, p. 17.

14   See Ehrlich: *Cinema of Paradox: French Filmmaking Under the German Occupation*, p. 14.

15   Bertin-Maghit, Jean-Pierre, *Le Cinéma français sous l'Occupation* (Paris: Presses Universitaires de France, 1994), p. 30.

16   NA, 'Le Juif Suss', *Le Film* 9 (15 February 1941), pp. 10–11; NA, 'Le Juif Suss: la presse est unanime', *Le Film* 11 (15 March 1941).

17   Rebatet, Lucien, *Les Tribus de cinéma et du théatre* (Paris: Nouvelles Editions Francaises, 1941); Harlé, P.-A., 'A propos des "Tribus du cinéma et du théâtre"', *Le Film* 17 (7 June 1941), p. 59.

18   Siclier: *La France de Pètain et son cinèma*, pp. 28–32.

19   Richebé, Roger, *Au-Delà de l'Écran: 70 ans de la vie d'un cinéaste* (Monte-Carlo: Editions Pastorelly, 1977), pp. 151–152.

20   Feuillère, Edwige, *Les Feux de la mémoire* (Paris: Albin Michel, 1977), p. 131.

21   Fonds Pierre Autré, BIFI Archives. *L'Activité Du Comité d'Organisation de l'Industrie Cinématographque* (Marked: Très Confidentiel), Confidential report on the activity of COIC. Five typescript pp., Fonds Pierre Autré (Paris, 17 July 1941).

22   Fonds Pierre Autré, BIFI Archives. *Reunion Des Collaborateurs de Création Du 14 Avril 1942*, Compte-rendues des séances; PA01 1942–1943 (14 Avril 1942).

23   Ibid.

24   Scholars disagree about how popular German films were in France. Evelyn Ehrlich argues that German films did not attract large audiences, and that financial losses made it more urgent for Continental to produce French films with recognisable actors. Jacques Siclier, while noting that they were never as popular as French films, nonetheless states that German films were popular in France. See Ehrlich: *Cinema of Paradox: French Filmmaking Under the German Occupation*, pp. 42–43; Siclier: *La France de Pétain et son cinéma*, pp. 19–20.

25   Ehrlich: *Cinema of Paradox: French Filmmaking Under the German Occupation*, p. 52.

26   Ehrlich: *Cinema of Paradox: French Filmmaking Under the German Occupation*, p. 53, p. 210 n.28.

27   Ehrlich also observes: 'If the French could be mollified with a relative liberalism of artistic expression, it was militarily and economically advantageous to encourage their best talents to produce the best possible effort', Ehrlich: *Cinema of Paradox: French Filmmaking Under the German Occupation*, p. 156.

28   *Le Corbeau* was not the only film of the Occupation to create a portrait of anonymous letter-writing. *Signé: Illisible* (1942) tells the tale of a series of kidnappings accompanied by anonymous letters. For a discussion of the film, see Burch, Noël and Geneviève Sellier, *La Drôle de guerre des sexes du cinéma français 1930–1956* (Paris: Nathan, 1996), pp. 128–129.

29   As Evelyn Ehrlich puts it: 'One obvious, but often forgotten point must be made at the outset: when the occupation began in 1940, no one knew it would only last four years. In fact, in 1940 it appeared likely than Germany would soon win the war and that France would be, indefinitely, an adjunct of the Third Reich', Ehrlich: *Cinema of Paradox: French Filmmaking Under the German Occupation*, p. xiii.

30   According to Pierre Billard, cinema revenues in Paris went from 452 million francs in 1938 down to 257 million in 1940, and then rose steadily: 416 million in 1941, 707 million in 1942 and 915 million in 1943. See *L'Age classique du cinéma français: Du cinéma parlant à la Nouvelle Vague* (Paris: Flammarion, 1995), p. 377.

31   Aurenche, Jean, *La Suite à l'Écran: Entretiens avec Anne et Alain Riou* (Lyon: Institut Lumière/Actes Sud, 1993), p. 109.

32   Burch and Sellier: *La Drôle de guerre des sexes du cinéma français 1930–1956*, p. 91.

33   Unless otherwise noted, biographical information about Clouzot is from Bocquet, José-Louis and Marc Godin, *Clouzot cinéaste* (Paris: Horizon Illimité, 2002).

34   Bocquet and Godin: *Clouzot cinéaste*, p. 14.

35   Bocquet and Godin: *Clouzot cinéaste*, p. 17.

36   Cited in Ehrlich: *Cinema of Paradox: French Filmmaking Under the German Occupation*, pp. 209–210 n.27.

37   Ehrlich cites an interview with Armand Panigel, in which he stated that the courtroom scene was actually directed by Clouzot after director Decoin refused to continue to work with Raimu. See Ehrlich: *Cinema of Paradox: French Filmmaking Under the German Occupation*, p. 209 n.27.

38   Duchâteau, André-Paul, and Stéphane Steeman, *L'Écrivain habite au 21: Stanislas-André Steeman* (Ottignies, Belgium: Quorum, 1998), p. 217.

39   The authors mention *L'Assassin habite au 21* as an example of boulevard cinema, very popular during the Occupation, which is generally misogynist and phallocentric. They note that some films reverse the stereotypes of the genre, particularly insofar as the 'crazy woman' who isn't crazy at all. See Burch and Sellier: *La Drôle de guerre des sexes du cinéma français 1930–1956*, p. 111.

40   R.D., 'Paris a accueilli triomphalement…L'Assassin habite au 21', *Miroir de L'Ecran* 13 (October 1942) p. 18.

41   Cited in Bocquet and Godin: *Clouzot cinéaste*, p. 29.

42   Suzy Delair, cited in Bocquet and Godin: *Clouzot cinéaste*, p. 27.

43   Fresnay, Pierre, and François Possot, *Pierre Fresnay* (Paris: Editions de la Table Ronde, 1975), p. 66.

44   See Chirat, Raymond, *Le Cinéma français des années de guerre* (Paris: Hatier/5 Continents, 1983), pp. 109–110.

45   Bocquet and Godin: *Clouzot cinéaste*, p. 30.

46   For details on the budget for costumes alone for *L'Assassin habite au 21*, see Bertin-Maghit: *Le Cinéma français sous l'Occupation* (Paris: Perrin, 1989; rpt. 2002), p. 122.

2 The film

Le Corbeau takes as its immediate central concern the assignation of guilt: who is the Raven, the author of the anonymous letters? But, as is almost always the case in a successful mystery, the process of discovery is as important as the final result. Thus, the search for the guilty party in the film becomes a search for other truths concerning desire and authority, and the anonymous letters reveal much about a community with secrets to hide. The very beginning of *Le Corbeau* is instructive in this regard, since it sets the tone for virtually everything that follows. The two opening scenes present the spectator with two different, but related introductions to the film. The film begins with a title: 'A little town, here or elsewhere.' We see a long shot of a tower on a hill, and the camera moves down and to the left to show us the small town. The camera pauses when the cemetery comes into view. A dissolve to a large archway takes us to the interior of what we will soon discover is the cemetery. The camera once again moves left, and the arches of the walkway frame our view of the cemetery. As the camera moves, the music accompanying the scene, which up to this point has been fairly standard, light fare, switches suddenly to become ominous, as if to suggest a malevolent presence. The flat lighting of the opening shot of the town is replaced by strong light and dark contrast. The camera moves quickly to frame the wrought-iron gate that provides a connection to the immediate outdoor area. The music suddenly stops, as the door opens noisily. The church spire and bell tower are again revealed through the open archway. Thus we are given two views of the church, one from a long shot overlooking the town, the other from the interior of the cemetery with the accompaniment of some kind of mysterious presence.

This prologue is a curious scene. Human presence is only implied; there are no actors present, no human movement, except for the opening of the wrought-iron door performed by an unseen hand. There is a palpable sense of unease created as the scene progresses. The prologue links the church with death; in both shots that comprise the film's beginning, the camera moves left, framing the church in both shots from different distances. While it is true that several key scenes in the film take place in a church, religion has an important role in *Le Corbeau* only to the extent that it is one of many institutions seen as potentially corrupt. More important is the way in which a sunny image of a seemingly picturesque town dissolves into images that suggest foreboding and anxiety, as if beneath every surface some trouble lurks. Not only will *Le Corbeau* show us trouble beneath the surface, it will also undo a number of cultural stereotypes concerning power, morality and authority.

After a dissolve to a country pasture where cows are grazing, the film provides us with a second expository scene that introduces us to the presumed hero of *Le Corbeau*, Dr Germain (played by Pierre Fresnay). In a country setting, three elderly women sit outdoors, waiting for news from Dr Germain. He emerges from the country house and tells one of the women that he saved the mother's life. Her immediate response is accusatory – 'Mon Dieu, docteur, vous n'avez pas fait ça' ('My God, doctor, you didn't do that') – and he is defensive as he warns that the woman's daughter must wait a time before attempting to become pregnant again. At the end of this scene, as Dr Germain drives off in his car, we hear the bells ringing from the church tower seen in the earlier prologue, thus providing a sound link between the two scenes Like the town itself, Dr Germain has his own secrets, eventually revealed to the spectator as the traumatic loss of his wife and son by an overzealous doctor who was determined (and who failed) to save the child's life at all costs.

After a further introduction to the town – children leave school for lunch, visitors enter the hospital – as well as to other key figures in the film, Dr Germain returns to the hospital, where he is confronted by a suspicious administrator who notes that he once again has saved the life of the mother (rather than that of the child). As the major and minor players in the film are introduced – Laura Vorzet, a social worker; Marie Corbin, a nurse and the sister of Laura; hospital administrators; a cancer patient; and his mother – it is clear that even before the mystery of the anonymous letters is presented as the central intrigue of the film, there is yet another mystery, and that is Dr Germain himself. He is presented as an outsider, a doctor whose preference for saving the life of the mother is considered suspicious. He takes no interest in the somewhat grisly fascination of his colleagues with a case of gangrene. He scolds the nurse Marie Corbin – who is herself presented as a bitter busybody – when he suspects she has stolen morphine. Yet if Germain is an outsider, the initial views we have of the hospital and its goings-on suggest that he is perhaps one voice of rationality in a world of corruption.

The first scenes in the hospital also reveal that there is a connection between the doctor and Laura Vorzet, a connection first suggested by Marie Corbin. Laura asks her sister why she is so disagreeable with the patients, and Marie retorts by asking Laura why she is so friendly with Dr Germain. This exchange is typical of the way in which information and exposition are presented in the film, through gossip, suspicion and surveillance (Marie says she knows why Laura spends so much time at the hospital and threatens to tell Laura's husband what is going on). While the circuit of knowledge may be unsavoury, Marie in this case is not wrong, and frequently in the film what appear to be rumours and false accusations have a basis of truth. Dr Germain and Laura, we soon discover, share a mutual attraction.

A study in oppositions

The early scenes of *Le Corbeau* follow Dr Germain through a series of encounters, from the birth to the hospital, and from the hospital to his residence in an apartment building overlooking a schoolyard. A series of bold oppositions is set up in these encounters. Indeed, *Le Corbeau* is a study in oppositions, apparent and real. In the prologue of the film, which moves quickly from a peaceful view of a town to a far more ominous view, we are introduced to the notion of a world off-balance, projecting contradictory images. In the course of the film, the use of shadows and light and dark contrast emphasise that sense of a menacing reality, of a world visible and mysterious at the same time. A particularly important sequence in this regard occurs when Germain enters the apartment building. Our first introduction to Denise occurs here (her brother, the schoolmaster, has asked Germain to look in on her since she has been complaining of illness). As Germain enters the foyer of the building and mounts the stairs, we see teenaged Rolande, playing with her ball, as she tells Germain he received a letter that she has left in his room. In the shot reverse shot between them, streaks of light through window grilles cast deep shadows (Figures 1, 2). Rolande may well seem a suspicious character simply by virtue of her presence as an omnipresent busy-body (thus she echoes Marie Corbin). But the fact that the entrance into this interior space is accompanied by a marked shift in light, from flat, exterior lighting (in the schoolyard) to this menacing realm of light and shadows, suggests trouble.

Figure 1: Light and shadows: Rémy Germain (Pierre Fresnay) in the stairwell.

Figure 2: Light and shadows: Rolande (Liliane Maigné) in the foyer.

When Germain enters Denise's room to examine her (and to discover that she is not ill, but interested in seducing him), the light/dark contrast is very much subdued, and Denise, in particular, is portrayed in flat, even lighting. Only when Laura shows up, on the pretext of bringing Denise some magazines but in fact to talk to Germain, does the lighting achieve the previous effects of high contrast and shadows. Germain and Laura move to the landing, and we see shadows of them projected against the wall as Laura tells him she has received an anonymous letter accusing her of being Germain's mistress (Figure 3). She tells him that she cannot see him any more, and, as she descends the stairs, the light and dark contrast is also heightened. As at the beginning of the scene, Rolande stands in wait like a sentry as Laura leaves the building. The scene concludes as we see Rolande, continuing to bounce her ball, and Germain, going into his room. Rolande quietly mounts the steps and peers through the keyhole to watch as Germain opens the letter.[1]

In this scene, the light and dark contrast creates a visual distinction between Denise, on the one hand, and Laura and Rolande, on the other, with Germain the only figure who moves from one space to another, from the foyer

Figure 3: Laura Vorzet (Micheline Francey) and Germain.

to Denise's room and back again. This scene embodies what is the most distinctive style of the film, the use of light and dark contrast and shadows to create a world of suspicion and paranoia. Ginette Vincendeau has explored the aesthetic of French film noir insofar as it is an important aspect of French film of the 1930s and 1940s, and several of the elements that she designates as central to the film noir world of Duvivier's *Pépé le Moko* (1937) are important in *Le Corbeau* as well: an 'expressionist use of *mise-en-scène* and its interaction of lighting, performance and décor' and 'a deep-rooted pessimism'.[2] While there are many examples of films noirs and film noir elements in French films of the 1930s, one of the overlooked aspects of Occupation cinema is the extent to which a film noir style worked in tandem with the preoccupation with crises of narrative authority and surveillance. There are noir elements in many films of the Occupation, particularly in those that mix genres, like *La Main du diable* and *L'Assassin habite au 21*. But as Vincendeau states, 'for genuine film noir during the Occupation, one has to turn to dramas such as Henri Decoin's adaptation of Simenon's *Les Inconnus dans la maison* (1942) and to *Le Corbeau* (1943)'.[3] One of Clouzot's, and *Le Corbeau*'s, distinct contributions to the cinema is precisely the masterful articulation of film noir as both an aesthetic and a point of view.

Between Denise and Laura, one would be hard-pressed to find a better example of the virgin and the whore dichotomy so typical of an entire tradition of female representation in the West: Denise is sexual, Laura is not; Denise wears a nightgown while Laura wears conservative dresses with tight necks; Denise is brunette, while Laura is blonde. The film adds a particularly interesting twist to this standard, if exaggerated, opposition, by staging the horizontal Denise against the vertical Laura! Denise spends the first part of the film quite literally in bed (Figure 4), and her physical affliction – the limp she has as a result of a car accident – is only visible when she emerges from bed, as if so startling a shift (from prone to vertical) required an equally striking physical manifestation. Laura, on the other hand, is first seen in the film upright, as she tends to her volunteer duties in the hospital, and then as she appears at the door to Denise's room (Figure 5). The contrasts between the two women are sustained, in the early scenes of the film, by the horizontal/vertical distinction, with the accompanying

Figure 4: Denise Saillens (Ginette Leclerc).

Figure 5: Laura at the door to Denise's room.

distinction that Laura is mobile while Denise is confined (willingly, but still confined) to her bed.

In a film preoccupied with deceit, it is no surprise that these scenes reveal deception, the most obvious of which is Denise's pretence of illness so that she can get close to Dr Germain. But there are none of the effects one might expect to cast Denise as a villain, particularly insofar as light and dark contrast is concerned. Rather, Denise's sexy bedroom pose is counterbalanced when we see Germain lean over her chest to listen to her breathing, and we see magazine pictures of movie stars arranged on her wall, as if she is a somewhat impressionable adolescent with a crush on the new resident of the building (Figure 6). But Laura is very much cast in these effects of light and dark contrast, despite the fact that her appearance and her presentation of herself as the victim of a malicious letter suggest a woman who has little to do with deception and malice. This, of course, is the film's secret, that the stereotypical image of female goodness is in fact something else altogether. For the time being, the introduction of Rolande, bouncing her ball and watching everyone around her, allows for a suspicion of guilt, while the opposition embodied by Denise and Laura is already becoming undone.

The character of Denise plays upon Ginette Leclerc's cinematic persona as a vamp, a *femme fatale* (her most famous role prior to *Le Corbeau* was as the unfaithful wife in Marcel Pagnol's *La Femme du boulanger/The Baker's Wife*, 1938). Yet the role of Denise, and the fact that she has a permanent limp, lends Leclerc's role an element of playing against type, particularly when she announces (to Germain, after they have slept together and he clearly is having second thoughts about their relationship): 'You've seen me limp because I was in my bare feet, but when I put on my shoes, no one notices a thing. I spent five years getting to that point. I did it, and I had all of the men I wanted, me, the cripple! And every time, I was avenging myself on life.' Raymond Chirat has pointed out that many actors in *Le Corbeau* – all of them well known to French audiences of the time – are played against type. Pierre Fresnay, as the sombre and haunted Germain, is a far cry from the dryly comical Wens of *Le Dernier des six* or *L'Assassin habite au 21*, and if he is

Figure 6: Denise and Germain in Denise's room.

considered a suspect (by the townspeople, and perhaps by spectators as well), his icy demeanour never really changes. Of Pierre Larquey, who plays Dr Vorzet, Chirat says that his 'traditional good-naturedness, emphasized by his umbrella, his bowler hat and his well-trimmed beard, disappears as events unfold'.[4] In other words, the manipulation of the personas of the actors contributes to the atmosphere of deceptive appearances and unexpected repressed desires in the film.

Laura, meanwhile, stands as the polar opposite of Denise. She may not be a mother, but she embodies the Aryan ideal of womanhood so visible in Vichy propaganda of the time.[5] In the course of the film, the roles of Denise and Laura are taken in unexpected directions, since Denise emerges from her *femme fatale* role – and her bed – as a presumably worthy companion to Dr Germain, while Laura's immaculate persona conceals a deeply disturbed woman who initiates the flood of anonymous letters. If the two women's roles are reversed in the film – the sexualised woman is really 'good', while the pure woman is really 'bad' – then other similarities between female characters speak not only to traditional stereotypes of women but also to their undoing. Two of the most likely villains in the film are the nurse Marie Corbin and the post office clerk Rolande. They share a strange kind of outsider status vis-à-vis sexuality – Rolande because she is younger than either Denise or Laura, Marie Corbin because she is older. But perhaps more important, they both embody a type – the surveilling female, obsessively interested in the affairs of others. Everyone watches everyone else in *Le Corbeau*, but in the case of these two female characters it is cause for a kind of pathology – and again, one that is undone in the film in the sense that they too are false leads.

Crises of narrative authority

If the women in *Le Corbeau* are part of a web of stark binary oppositions that are put into question in the course of the film, Dr Germain too is located within a binary opposition, as both the opposite and the parallel of Dr Vorzet. Immediately after Germain has read the first anonymous letter, which accuses him of 'messing around' with Laura Vorzet, there is a dissolve to the interior of the Vorzet residence, where Laura walks through the door with her husband, who has just returned from a medical conference. In parallel to the preceding scene in Germain's room, Laura discovers an anonymous letter in the mailbox addressed to her husband. If Dr Germain appears to be a central narrative authority in the film, a logical assumption since his actions drive most of the opening scenes, the film now moves to a different level of narration by creating connections between the two male doctors.

Dr Germain is an enigmatic individual, yet he is also the central link between the opening scenes of the film, from the child's death in the countryside to the hospital, and from the hospital to the schoolyard and the apartment building. With the introduction of Dr Vorzet, another level of narration is introduced, one that regards Germain from the vantage point of his similarities to and differences from Dr Vorzet. Both men are connected to Laura, and they are both doctors. They are the first visible recipients of anonymous letters. But Vorzet is an old man, and while he constantly holds forth with philosophical and medical observations, Germain is reticent and rarely if ever talks about himself or his opinions. Sometimes when we see Germain and Vorzet together, in the same frame, they appear as two professionals exchanging words (with Vorzet exchanging far more than Germain does). But the striking use of contrast and shadows also affords us evocative looks at the two men, suggesting that the link between the two of them has to do with fundamental questions of power and desire. When, for example, Dr Vorzet comes to see Germain and to warn him that the forces of suspicion are closing in on him (and to do a bit of nosing around of his own), the scene concludes (as do so many of the provocative scenes in the film) on the landing of Germain's apartment building. As Vorzet walks down the steps and away from Germain, the man's shadow remains while he moves out of frame, a looming, haunting reminder both of Germain's own secrets and of the power we eventually recognise as Vorzet's desire (Figure 7).

The culmination of the relationship between the two doctors occurs in the most famous scene in the film. While far more space in the film, both visually and narratively, is devoted to the binary oppositions embodied by women, the most explicit discussion *about* opposition occurs between Germain and Vorzet. The scene takes place in the schoolroom after Vorzet has led the dictation session. The room is dark, and a ceiling lamp and a globe are visible. Dr Vorzet tells Dr Germain his view of the world: 'You believe that people are either completely good or completely evil! You believe that goodness is light, and evil is darkness. But where is the darkness? Where is the light?' He performs this discourse on the impossibility of dividing the world into black and white by swinging the lamp so that sharp light and dark contrast characterises the scene in a literal illustration of his words. The nature of opposition is theorised and staged simultaneously. Vorzet prefaces his remarks with the confession that he is a drug addict, and that Marie Corbin stole drugs from the hospital for his benefit (they used to be lovers and were once engaged to be married). Vorzet seems to articulate what amounts to a compelling point of view for the film as a whole, and a common assumption is that this scene does indeed embody the philosophy of the entire film. There is no question that this scene is central to the film. It offers an explicitly philosophical and moral discussion, and it reads easily as an overarching commentary, standing over the film just as persuasively as Vorzet manipulates the light source. Yet it is difficult to take any discourse at face

Figure 7: Germain and Vorzet's (Pierre Larquey) shadow.

value in *Le Corbeau*. In this particular instance, Vorzet's comments function ironically – i.e., his discourse is enormously self-serving, and his notions of moral relativism notwithstanding, they provide a way of shielding his guilt.

As distinctive as the globe scene is, it finds a mirror image of sorts in another scene that stands out from the rest of the film. During the procession through the town for the funeral of 'number 13', the patient who kills himself once he receives an anonymous letter telling him that his disease is fatal, another anonymous letter falls from the funeral wreath. The scene creates a mounting sense of tension and anger, largely through a series of low-angle shots at increasingly close range, showing us a town official who holds forth with pompously delivered clichés about the tragedy of the man's death; the victim's mother, shrouded in black; and different members of the community, including, in particular, Marie Corbin. The crowd becomes increasingly agitated, particularly insofar as Marie Corbin is concerned; she was already considered suspicious, and her very appearance at the procession was taken by some as a provocation.

The first individual publicly (and erroneously, as we discover shortly) identified as the 'Raven' is Marie Corbin, and the scene is significant for its demonstration of the violent eagerness with which the townspeople seek a culprit. The funeral procession scene also stages a dramatic contrast between two women, the nurse, Marie Corbin, presumed to be guilty, and the mother, presented in her black mourning dress and veil as an icon of female suffering. Stylistically, the funeral scene – particularly insofar as its sharp, low angles are concerned – prefigures the globe scene. The shift into another register of cinematic representation in both scenes accentuates the function of the schoolroom scene as a discursive centre for the film as a whole, for, in mirroring, style-wise, the earlier scene, it offers itself as a meditation on it. Yet, however much the two scenes evoke one another, there is also a distinct difference between them. The funeral scene is noisy, both in terms of the pretentious discourse of the town official and the noise of the crowd, while the classroom scene between Vorzet and Germain is, in contrast, a meditative scene. Thus if the schoolroom scene is a privileged site for theoretical reflection, it would seem to follow the age-old rule of classical cinema: women may occupy the visual plane, but men control it.

However, I think it is a mistake to leave Vorzet's discourse, with the sharp contrast of black and white, the swinging globe and the shifting shadows, as a kind of master discourse in the film. Just as this scene can be seen in parallel to the earlier funeral scene, virtually every person and every event in *Le Corbeau* has a double or a mirror of some kind. The classroom scene is not the resolution of a parallel, but rather it too receives two replies in the scenes that follow.

After Vorzet leaves Germain in the school classroom, a dissolve from the swinging lamp to a still one marks the passage of time. It is the next day, and Germain has fallen asleep at the teacher's desk. He is startled by the arrival of the mother of the suicide victim, who tells him that she now works as a cleaning woman at the school. This woman also manipulates light and shadow, although not in the dramatic way that Vorzet does. She approaches the window, and opens the curtains, so that she and Germain are framed by the window and situated in the morning light. She tells Germain that she is fairly certain who is responsible for the anonymous letters, and that she is waiting for the right moment to attack, at which point she takes out her son's

Figure 8: Germain during Gemain and Vorzet's discussion of good and evil.

Figure 9: Vorzet during Germain and Vorzet's discussion of good and evil.

straight razor, with which he killed himself. Shadows are visible, but the lighting is much flatter than in the previous scene, and the conversation less dramatic because there is no manipulation of the light to compare with the swinging lamp. Nor are there any sharp angles to compare with the previous scene. Rather, the conversation between the two is filmed straightforwardly, moving from a two-shot of them in front of the window, to a shot reverse shot, in which we see each of them in medium close-up. These close-ups mark a significant shift from the previous conversation between Vorzet and Germain (Figures 8, 9), for we see Germain and the woman at much closer range than was the case with the two male doctors (Figures 10, 11). The casting of the mother is significant here as well, for the actress Sylvie had, only a few months before the opening of *Le Corbeau*, played the role of the Mother Superior in Robert Bresson's film *Les Anges du péché*. However coincidental the evocation of the earlier role, through dress in particular, the parallel suggests her function as avenging angel in whom revenge and purity coexist.

After his conversation with the woman, Germain goes to Denise's apartment, where he discovers her anonymous letter to him. Denise is not in

Figure 10: The mother of the hospital patient (Sylvie) during her conversation with Germain.

Figure 11: Germain during his conversation with the mother of the hospital patient.

her room when Germain arrives, so he hides until she returns and then confronts her. Denise insists that she did not know any other way to tell Germain of her pregnancy. Denise tells Germain to look into her eyes to discover the truth of her innocence. In contrast to Vorzet's relativism, Denise does divide the world into the opposing camps of intellect and feeling, and offers her face as a sign of truth. Yet unlike the mother, who has ensured her right to avenge the death of her son, there is not at all the same tone of certainty in Denise's words. It's a curious scene, for the close-ups of Denise's face, with her trembling lips and tearful eyes, and those of Germain, with his eyes wide in apparent astonishment, convey little of the absolute truth that Denise suggests (Figures 12, 13). In this exchange between Germain and Denise, we see extreme close-ups of their faces (comparable extreme close-ups are not used elsewhere in the film), so that virtually any other object within the frame is invisible. Vorzet asserts ambiguity with certainty; Denise asserts certainty in an ambiguous way. In both cases, the encounter provokes a dramatic shift in cinematic representation – extreme light and dark and extreme angles in the case of Vorzet and Germain, and extreme close-ups in the case of Denise and Germain.

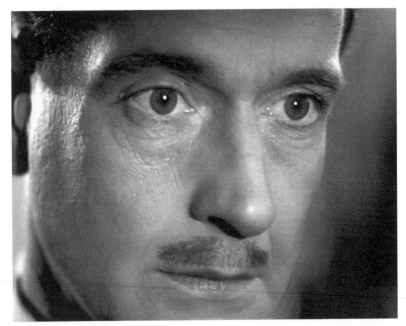

Figure 12: Germain in extreme close-up during his conversation with Denise.

Figure 13: Denise in extreme close-up during her conversation with Germain.

And what of the mother of the suicide victim? As befits her position as a mediator between Vorzet and Denise in this sequence of scenes, she possesses a certainty that shares characteristics with both Vorzet and Denise, and which is different at the same time. Each of these conversations focuses on the nature of truth, from Vorzet's elaborate staging of the light and shadows of his demonstration on relativity, to the mother's blunt insistence, in the bright natural light of morning, that revenge is hers to take, to Denise's emphatic insistence on her innocence and Germain's inability to live in the world of sensation and emotion. Each of these conversations amounts to a challenge to Germain's way of being in the world. In the case of Vorzet and Denise, these challenges evoke drastic changes in the look of the film, thus calling attention to the scenes but also suggesting their difference from what surrounds them. Vorzet presents his skill as a *metteur-en-scène*, while Denise presents her face, thus evoking a classically patriarchal division – the man sets the scene, the woman offers her body. But, in order for this sexual division of the world to work, Germain has to assume his position as recipient and interpreter of the older man's knowledge, and/or as heterosexual love object of the woman who offers her face as proof of her purity. I suggest that despite his visibility in these scenes, Germain does not assume the positions of narrative authority required of him.

Wedged as it is between the far more dramatic encounters between Vorzet and Germain, and Germain and Denise, it is easy to pass over the scene between the mother and Germain. The scene is evocative of the second 'prologue' of the film, when Germain saves the mother rather than the child. Close-ups portray him and the old woman (the mother of the pregnant woman) as he dispenses his advice (Figures 14, 15). If Germain's authority was affirmed at the beginning of the film, here it has weakened considerably. But the exchange between Germain and the mother of the cancer victim provides the framework for the concluding images of the film. Here, in the schoolroom, the woman walks toward Germain at the desk; at the end of the film, Germain looks up from Vorzet's desk and watches her depart. Here, she announces her intentions to Germain's horror; then, she commits the act that allows Germain – finally – to understand that Vorzet was guilty.

Arguably the two women – Denise and the mother – are far more adept than Germain at solving the mystery of the Raven's identity. Germain is convinced that Denise is the culprit, and then when he discovers Laura's apparent guilt, he is just as certain of her total responsibility for the crime. Denise intuits what the mother of the suicide victim knows, that someone else was responsible. We are not privy to how the mother deduces Vorzet's guilt, but we know that Denise senses Laura's fear too much to believe that she could be totally responsible. Is this a classic example of women's intuition, marshalled here to demonstrate the failures of male rationalism, of logic, of reason? While Germain's powers of deduction fail him, the film makes a telling connection between the three conversations I have described, each underscoring Germain's increasing inability to hear, to listen, to comprehend.

Feminist analyses of shot reverse shot across a wide range of films have demonstrated the extent to which the assertion of cinematic patriarchal authority relies upon the staging of the man as the privileged source of sight, and the woman as object of the look. Each of these conversations concludes with one of the most standard, classical modes of point of view and authority in the cinema, the shot reverse shot construction. The extreme close-up of

Denise would appear to be a clichéd example of the woman's status in her 'to-be-looked-atness', for her face fills the frame, offering itself to her male lover.[6] But Germain fails utterly to acquire the authority, cinematic or narrative, that is thrust upon him. The image of his face may well fill the frame, but he does not assume a position of authority, of the privileged male gaze. Rather, Germain departs from the conversation with Vorzet only to be overwhelmed by the mother's plan for revenge and by Denise's declarations. These scenes do not allow Germain to establish authority, but rather suggest the threatening possibility that the two women are far more capable of narrative and visual authority than he is.

This sequence of scenes initiates the resolution of the film – or, rather, the lack of resolution. Despite the reputation of Le Corbeau as a stunning thriller, the resolution of the film in its final scenes is perplexing. Vorzet is revealed as the Raven, but the revelation occurs very quickly, and it is not as though Laura is blameless. She admits that she wrote the first letters, and she claims Vorzet forced her to write the remaining ones. Noël Burch and Geneviève Sellier, noting the inconsistencies in the film's conclusion, say that

Figure 14: The mother of the pregnant woman in conversation with Germain.

'uncertainty remains concerning the sharing of responsibility within this "infernal couple".'[7] While the exact roles played by each do remain unknown, I do not think we need to search for the resolution of this enigma, as Burch and Sellier do, by claiming that the confusing ending of the film is only a screen for the 'real' authors of the anonymous letters – Clouzot and Chavance. For in placing blame on both the man and the woman, the film introduces an element of indecidability, of ambiguity, not primarily about who did what, but about gender and its relationship to agency and authority. For the supremely patriarchal figure of Vorzet is as corrupt and deranged as the woman who looks like a Vichy poster for womanhood but acts like a lunatic. And as for the man who supposedly emerges from the depths of hell to assume his identity as a heterosexual and a father: Germain's 'transformation' seems to me far more ambiguous than the solution to the letter-writer's identity. True, Germain opens the windows of Denise's room to welcome the voices of the children outside, and he seems to accept her pregnancy. What he says, however, is not exactly a ringing endorsement of the heterosexual plot. When Denise asks, 'Would you kill me to ensure the birth of your son?'

Figure 15: Germain in conversation with the mother of the pregnant woman.

Germain replies: 'Perhaps...' However much one might want to make these closing words a reflection of pro-natalist ideology (as Burch and Sellier argue), they work more to leave this newly formed couple in a decidedly ambiguous place. And throughout the final scenes of the film, Germain possesses the same look of stunned incomprehension as he did when faced with the trembling lips and watering eyes of Denise. Germain's function, as a spectator within the film, is to register increasing confusion when faced with the certitude of a mother's desire for revenge and of a woman's certainty about love and emotion. True, he announces the final words of the film – 'Thus it was Vorzet' – to make clear the guilt of the psychiatrist. But the conclusion of the film does not really belong to him, except in his role as spectator; it belongs to the mother, and to a lesser extent, to Denise. In other words, then, Le Corbeau's 'conclusion' is the possibility of a world where gender confusion reigns; where women know, understand and act in the absence of any viable male authority.

From Tulle to St-Robin

The evolution of the script for Le Corbeau reflects important assumptions about the relationship between narrative authority, gender and crime. The history of the writing of Le Corbeau is a tale of assumptions about gender and narration that shape the film generally, and, more specifically, the various threads that intertwine at the film's conclusion. Louis Chavance's major defence, when faced with the charges against Le Corbeau, was that he had written a first version of the screenplay in 1933, and that in 1937 he had deposited the screenplay with the Association des Auteurs de Films. Hence, the film could hardly be seen as complicit with the German occupiers, according to Chavance, and in addition, Clouzot and Chavance both argued that the film criticises the practice of anonymous letter-writing. It is well known that anonymous letters of denunciation flourished during the Second World War in France, and that for the German occupiers, anonymous letters provided a significant source of information about the black market, about Jewish residents and about Resistance activities. Simply to assert that anonymous letters flourished in Occupied France, however, can be a somewhat deceptive and superficial way of situating the film in its historical context. While anonymous letters may well have been a fact of life in Occupied France, the practice was not always as encouraged by the German occupiers and the officials of Vichy as some accounts would lead one to believe. The letters provided tips, to be sure, but just as often they were motivated by petty jealousy and personal vendettas.[8]

The proliferation of anonymous letters stands as symptomatic of one of the many paradoxes of Vichy, Nazi Occupation and collaboration. For anonymous letters of denunciation could well have been seen as perpetuating the dreaded image of France as a weak, feminised adversary of Germany, not brave or strong enough to stand up to the invader either in battle or in daily life. The practice of anonymous letter-writing corresponds to the worst stereotypes of devious, gossiping, feminine behaviour. Vichy officials and French collaborators were determined to combat the image of a feminised, passive France. But the sneaky, passive/aggressive mode of anonymous letter-writing affirms the stereotype. Paradoxically, of course, it was a stereotype upon which the collaborationists and occupiers relied, within limits.

Whether or not one accepts Chavance's and Clouzot's claim that the film is 'against' the practice of anonymous letter-writing, it is certain that for viewers of the film, the most immediate point of reference was the situation of Occupied France, and the frenzy that besets the fictional town of Saint-Robin provides a parallel to the experience of Occupation. But the connection between the film and Occupied France via the anonymous letters can obscure what is one of the most interesting aspects of the evolution of the screenplay of the film. Chavance was inspired by an epidemic of anonymous letters that occurred in the town of Tulle, beginning in 1917. He wrote the screenplay using various news sources, but most important were the writings by Edmond Locard, a police official and a psychiatrist, who investigated and solved the Tulle case.[9]

Louis Chavance's first draft, entitled 'L'oeil de serpent', dated 1932, recounts a story that is both like and unlike Clouzot's film. A small French town is inundated with a series of anonymous letters. Dr Monatte, a new doctor in town, is having difficulty establishing a practice because he is perceived as young and has progressive ideas about medicine. His wife, Denise, receives an anonymous letter claiming that Dr Monatte had an affair with, and performed an abortion on, Laura Doret, a young mother who has decided to stay in her home town while her husband works as a colonial functionary in Africa. Denise believes the letter, since her husband has been treating Laura for her 'troubles nerveux'. Monatte is arrested, but he is released when the letters continue despite his incarceration. The volume of anonymous letters magnifies. Since Monatte finds himself ostracised by the hospital when he attempts to return to work after his arrest, he begins to investigate the matter himself. He immediately suspects a nurse, who is the only person at the hospital spared by the poison pen, and his suspicions are only multiplied by the fact that the woman is homely and cross-eyed. In an episode that will remain central to Clouzot's otherwise considerable reworking of the screenplay, a cancer patient of the nurse receives a letter saying that his disease is fatal, and he promptly kills himself with a straight razor. At the man's funeral, the nurse's own sister-in-law, Laura (the nurse is the sister of Laura's husband), accuses the nurse. But Monatte no longer believes in the nurse's guilt and he protects her.

The letters achieve epidemic proportions. Local authorities are convinced that there are at 20 twenty letter-writers, but they also know that 'l'oeil de serpent' – the instigator's pen-name – is the source, as well as the most vicious letter-writer of all. The letters will stop, they are certain, once this individual is caught. The tension continues to mount and the entire town is obsessed by the anonymous letters. One day Denise tells Monatte that at the market, she overheard that another doctor at the hospital was denounced in a letter as an abortionist. But when Monatte makes a comment to this colleague later in the day, the fellow doctor is stunned, for he had quite literally just received the letter. How could Monatte have known? Fearing of course that the veil of suspicion is once more falling upon him, Monatte rushes to Denise to ask her who spoke of the letter – it was Laura Doret. When Monatte confronts Laura, she denies the accusation that she is the serpent's eye. But Monatte sees, on the desk blotter, the imprint of the handwriting of the letter-writer, and goes to the police. Laura at last confesses to him, but offers this justification: her husband has returned from Africa and has been living with her in secret; he has been driven crazy by tropical disease and he threatened to kill Laura if she did not agree to write the letters. She points to a window in a door, where indeed a man's silhouette can be seen walking back and forth. Monatte is confused, and leaves. In the last scene of Chavance's first screenplay, Laura laughs hysterically as she watches her son in the next room; he parades a life-size puppet back and forth across the room.

In another, somewhat later version of the screenplay, Chavance makes the ending even clearer: Monatte, when he confronts Laura, hears a male voice call her name. He returns a few moments later and finds her dead, poisoned. The truth is finally told (although Chavance does not specify how), that Laura's husband died in the colonies, and she invented the story of his return to cover up her own guilt as the serpent's eye. The voice belonged not to Laura's husband, but rather to a neighbour calling her.

In yet another later version of the screenplay, other details are added: the character of Dr Vorzet is introduced as Laura's father; Laura's husband is still in the colonies. Laura is no longer the villain, but rather it is Vorzet, Laura's father, who is unmasked as the perpetrator. As in Clouzot's final version of the film, the mother of the cancer patient kills him with the same knife her son used to kill himself. This version of the screenplay is quite close to the final film, although it required yet another version of the screenplay for Vorzet to be identified as Laura's husband, not her father, with the husband in the colonies finally banished from the script.[10]

Of the changes that Clouzot made to Chavance's original story, five stand out as particularly striking. First and foremost, the identity of the villain changes, from Laura to Vorzet. In Clouzot's film, Laura is the 'false conclusion', the lure, but Vorzet is revealed, finally, to be the ultimate culprit. Second, while the changes undergone by the character of Denise are less striking, they are crucial, for in Clouzot's final film, Denise may be many things, but she is definitely not bourgeois, as she is described in Chavance's screenplay. Once Dr Monatte is given a past with the tragic death of a wife, Denise is free, as it were, to be the other woman, rather than Monatte's wife, in Clouzot's film. Third, a new character is added to the final film, Rolande, the pre-pubescent post office worker, who mirrors Marie Corbin. Fourth, while abortion is certainly present in the earliest version of Chavance's screenplay, it doesn't have the same importance it does in the final film. In Clouzot's film, no one aside from Dr Monatte (now using the pseudonym of Dr Germain) is accused of performing abortions, so that the suspicion of abortion contributes far more heavily to the characterisation of Dr Germain in the film.

Fifth and finally, one of the distinctive features of Chavance's screenplay, even into the final version of the film script, is the pronounced emphasis on the epidemic quality of the poison pen letters. In virtually every version of the screenplay, attention is drawn to the fact that there may well be one central culprit, but that the writing of the letters spreads across the town like a contagious virus.[11] While there is no question that a frenzy seizes the town in Clouzot's film, only briefly is it suggested that letter-writing has moved beyond the activities of the Raven. The letters reveal what is repressed and feared in the town, and in that sense are a powerful catalyst, but there is not the same strong sense that all the villagers have been overpowered by the desire to write poison pen letters. True, there is a scene at the post office in the final film where the epidemic quality of the anonymous letters is discussed, but it is quite subdued in comparison to Chavance's earlier drafts. In this context, Denise's desperate decision to write a fake letter appears all the more striking. In other words, in the absence of the stress on the epidemic quality of poison pen letters, individual pathology is emphasised even more strongly.[12]

In order to appreciate fully the range of the changes that Clouzot made to Chavance's script, and in order to understand why those changes are so significant in terms of the place of gender in Le Corbeau, we need to look more closely at the inspiration for Chavance's screenplay. For Clouzot adapted not only a screenplay but a legend. As I've noted, Chavance was inspired by the events that began in 1917 in the small town of Tulle. The anonymous letters that flooded the town were full of accusations – which in some cases were true – about adulterous love affairs, political intrigues and other details of the private lives of its citizens. At least a thousand letters were written over a span of three years, and their impact was all the more strong given, that like many small towns in France during the First World War, a good portion of its male residents had gone to war.[13]

The culprit was clever. Once surveillance of mailboxes began, the letter-writer dropped letters in churches, in market baskets and in the street. The letter-writer seemed to have a wealth of knowledge about the inhabitants of the town. One anonymous letter, found by a young boy in the street, provided a chart listing married couples and their lovers. Another letter, addressed to a Mme de Martin, informed the society woman in question that the 'de' in her name was acquired falsely, and proceeded to tell a tale about the crimes of the woman's great-grandfather; then threatened to send letters to all of the woman's acquaintances if she did not immediately remove the 'de' from her name. Mme de Martin panicked, for the story – which she thought safely ensconced in the past – was true. A frequent theme of the letters sent to the wives of soldiers was detailed and obscene descriptions of the husbands' sexual activities while away. The letters had a kind of mesmerising effect on the town; they provided an ongoing melodrama, either by playing upon long-existing rivalries or by introducing new items of gossip. But when a man died after receiving an anonymous letter, supposedly from his wife, confessing to infidelities and describing her own suicide, it was decided that more serious action was required. (Two stories circulated about the man's death – one that he shot himself as soon as he received the letter, the second that he was committed to a mental institution and died shortly after.)[14]

From 1917 to 1921, even though virtually all of the residents of the town had been affected by the anonymous letter-writer, no one knew who was responsible. Finally, in 1921, Jean Laval, a bureau chief and archivist, decided to pursue legal means to try to find the guilty party. Through a series of events worthy of the best detective story, it became apparent that whoever was writing the letters had privileged access to archival information, not just gossip about the various unsavoury pasts and presents of the inhabitants. For the letters often revealed knowledge that could have come only from court and municipal records. The judge in charge of the case, M. Richard, began to suspect none other than Jean Laval himself. At this point an expert was brought in on the case, Edmond Locard, director of the police laboratory in Lyon and something of an expert on '*anonymographie*' – anonymous letter-writing.

The first break in the case came when Jean Laval reported to the judge that a woman of his acquaintance had received a letter and had reported its contents to Laval's sister, Angèle. Richard discovered that the woman had received the letter on a Friday, but Angèle had described its contents to her brother two days before. Suspicion was cast, then, on Angèle Laval. Dr Locard subjected Angèle to a lengthy dictation session, beginning with the letter that had just been sent. Angèle wrote slowly, as if attempting to invent a new style of writing for herself; Locard recognised her attempt to stall for time, and put pressure on her to speed up. Angèle became increasingly distraught, and Locard threatened to take her to a hospital and perform gynaecological surgery if she didn't calm down! And so she did, continuing to write for hours, until finally her handwriting became identical to that of the poison pen letters. Yet Laval continued to maintain her innocence. During the ensuing trial, Laval's lawyers claimed that Laval was far too well brought up to commit such crimes, and noted in particular that the letters were so full of pornographic detail, so obscene, that it was impossible to imagine where Angèle Laval would have obtained such information. Laval was found guilty, but her sentence was relatively light – a one-month suspended jail sentence and numerous fines.

According to Dr Locard, who was an expert in both anonymous letters and handwriting analysis, Angèle Laval met virtually every criterion that characterised poison pen letter-writers. First and foremost, Laval was female; virtually all cases of l'anonymographie were women. In the old days, according to Locard, they would have been classified as 'hysterics' (interestingly, Locard himself was not above using the diagnosis of 'hysteria'). Laval initially wrote the letters in cahoots with family members, especially her mother; only later did Laval become the principal author. She wrote thousands of letters. An epidemic quality was attained as the letters by Laval set loose a frenzy of accusations and other anonymous letters. Laval was from the proverbial 'good family', as were all letter-writers (according to Locard's analysis), but suffered from a lack of attention and an overreaction to a romantic slight (she and a co-worker competed for the attentions of their boss). Laval had sent an anonymous letter to her boss, and then told him about receiving one herself accusing her of having an affair with him. Laval's attempt to forge a connection between her and her boss misfired, for he soon married Laval's co-worker. Laval thus devised a plan to cast suspicion on the couple. Such a preoccupation with sexuality and romantic intrigue was again a common characteristic of these letter-writers, according to Locard.[15]

The two primary actors in the Tulle affair, for the purposes of *Le Corbeau*, are Angèle Laval and Edmond Locard. Given the differences between Chavance's screenplays and the final film, one could easily assume that Clouzot turned a 1920s story into a 1940s film – that is, transformed the primarily psychological tale of anonymous letter-writing into a more topical one, made to the measure of a different time where anonymous letters had an entirely different meaning. But Clouzot too was influenced directly by the Laval case. There are features of the Tulle affair that were not included by Chavance in his original screenplays, but which did emerge in the final version of the film.

Three of these features are particularly important. First, in the early scenes of the film, Laura and Germain meet because both have received anonymous letters, and only at the end of the film do we realise that Laura wrote the letters. Laura thus imitates Angèle Laval's initiation into anonymous letter-writing, when she used the letters to pursue a romance with her boss. Second, if it is unclear, at the end of Clouzot's film, what the division of labour is between Vorzet and Laura in the writing of the letters, this is in fact reflective of an aspect of *l'anonymographie* emphasised by Locard, but not Chavance – that the letter-writing almost always begins as a family affair, until one person takes over (Locard stressed that the primary author was female). Finally, the most striking reference to the Tulle case in *Le Corbeau* is the dictation session, for the scene is a direct reference to Locard's dramatic discovery of Angèle Laval's guilt. Now Clouzot may cite aspects of the Laval case, but the results are quite different from Chavance's screenplays. Laura's disclosure to Germain of the anonymous letter she has received does not misfire, as it did with Laval; it seems rather to produce the effect so desired by Laval (and Laura), to intensify the attraction between her and the man she loved. The dictation session, which was a bravura demonstration of Locard's expertise in the Laval case, turns out to be a massive screen, as it were, for Vorzet, for the authority of the expert is put on display and then, later, undermined when it is revealed that the quest for the culprit leads to him.

Chavance's tale, in all of its versions, reads like a case history *à la* Locard. Edmond Locard is a kind of implicit narrator of Chavance's screenplays, for his theories on anonymous letter-writers form the substance of the script: Laura is as perfect a suspect as Angèle Laval, for she is female, from a 'good home', preoccupied with sexual matters and 'hysterical'. Some of her worst attacks are for herself – a typical strategy, according to Locard. But Clouzot takes an entirely different approach – virtually all of Dr Vorzet's theorising becomes a way of deflecting suspicion away from himself. The man of science, in interpreting and theorising the causes of mental illness, is in fact interpreting himself. The expert may well stand back and evaluate the behaviour of himself and others, but this does not ensure his innocence; in fact, any possibility of marking a line between the guilty and the innocent is undone. By casting Dr Vorzet as Locard, Clouzot undermines the interpretive authority that was so central to Chavance's screenplays.

The *Affaire de Tulle*, as it was called, received enormous attention in the French press. During Laval's trial, journalists from cities all over France were

Figure 16: Shadows and phantoms: Denise, Germain and an unidentified shadow.

in attendance. Laval's case of *l'anonymographie* did not only inspire imitators in the town of Tulle, but in other towns as well, and Locard reported being much in demand after the Laval case to solve similar cases. But it is impossible to say whether the case of Angèle Laval would have been an immediate point of reference for spectators in 1943, more than 20 years after the *Affaire de Tulle*. And given that anonymous letters had a much more immediate point of reference, namely the Occupation and the surveillance they implied, one suspects that Angèle Laval was of secondary importance in the reception of *Le Corbeau*. Angèle Laval was not Christine or Léa Papin, or Violette Nozière, famous female criminals of the 1930s whose exploits have remained highly visible over the years. Yet enough of Angèle Laval's story remains in Clouzot's film to justify the retracing of the 1943 film back to the events that began in 1917.

Despite all of the echoes of Tulle that remain in *Le Corbeau*, the change of the letter-writer from a woman to a man is the most striking and dramatic change. Why the gender switch? Burch and Sellier note that the mocking of patriarchal authority was central to many films of the Occupation, and so this unmasking of Vorzet would appear to be consistent with other films of the era.[16] The figure of patriarchal authority is not only mocked; he is feminised. As an *anonymographe*, Vorzet displays a collapse of authority, knowledge and manhood. As Burch and Sellier point out, Pierre Larquey was well known for playing the role of the weak father figure in films of the Occupation.[17] Larquey has a hangdog look about him and a passive demeanour; the conclusion of the film returns the actor to the 'type' with which he was most associated. As I've already suggested, I do not think Germain can be seen as occupying the void left by Vorzet's feminisation. Cinematically, Germain can hardly function in a shot reverse shot as the bearer of the look; narratively, he fails to read the clues that surround him. When we look closely at the conclusion of the film, two figures emerge in a mirror-like symmetry to fill the void – Denise and the mother.

Before Denise can assume this function as reflection to the avenging angel embodied by the mother, she has to pass a test of sorts: an attempted miscarriage (put another way, an abortion), one of many events that arrive quickly at the conclusion of the film (when Germain is at the Vorzet home, after the supposed realisation of Laura's guilt, Vorzet receives a phone call with the information that Denise has just fallen down the steps; she later tells Germain that she did it on purpose). The mother may avenge successfully her son's death, and Denise may fail in her attempted miscarriage, but both women must be marked as criminal. It has been noted that abortion is one of the most prevalent markers of the film's situation in the Occupation, and that its presence is surely one of the reasons for the controversy the film provoked.[18] Yet abortion has a curious presence in the film.

We are introduced to Germain after he has committed what is, technically and according to the prevailing ideology of Vichy, an abortion – he saves the mother's life rather than the child's. In the early scenes of the film, much is said *about* abortion without ever saying the words *avorter* or *avorteur*, which are uttered well after the preoccupation with abortion has been established. Rather, the word *avorter* is a perturbing signifier in the film. The very name of the villain of the film – Vorzet – echoes and masks simultaneously the word *avorter* in French. The name is first spoken when the cancer patient asks Laura if she is indeed 'la femme du Docteur Vorzet ("the wife of Doctor Vorzet")'. The first anonymous letter we see in the film (as read by Germain) is displayed for the camera, and we see the phrase: 'tu fais joujou avec la femme à Vorzet' ('you're messing around with Vorzet's wife'). The simple shift in prepositions creates a linguistic slippage, so that the simple pronunciation of the name 'Vorzet', and in particular, 'la femme à Vorzet', alludes to the word *avorter*. Vorzet by his very name, and Germain by his supposedly suspicious activities, bear the mark of abortion. Since the theme of abortion is so often cited as a way of defining the film in its historical context, it is then appropriate to recall that abortion was not commonly associated with men during the Occupation. It was primarily a woman's crime, and it was primarily women who were prosecuted for performing abortions.[19] Vorzet is the primary example in the film of the feminisation of men – as a writer of anonymous letters, he performs what is standardly a woman's crime, and his name recalls yet another crime associated with women. But Germain cannot escape from the taint of womanhood either.

The point here is not to claim a pro-natalist ideology for the film, for the way in which the signifier of 'abortion' is presented in the film cannot sustain the weight of such a clearly defined ideological agenda. The evocation of abortion, like the male appropriation of the 'female' crime of anonymous letter-writing, create a universe where men can no longer act like men, can no longer be like men. What's left are the women who also 'speak' through their crimes. In the context of occupied France, this is a pessimistic portrait of a world gone gender-berserk. With the hindsight of history, it is a masterful yet deeply patriarchal attempt to demonstrate the consequences of what happens when women speak. Like other films made during the Occupation, *Le Corbeau* is preoccupied with crises of gender and male authority, but its status as a 'representative' film will always be complicated by the fact that it functions so brilliantly on so many levels at once, from its explorations of gender and narrative authority to its evocation of a film noir atmosphere, from its phenomenal characterisations of players who both embody and exceed the 'types' they play to the unsettling sense that every seemingly clear-cut opposition can come undone.

Le Corbeau is a deeply pessimistic film, and it stands apart not only from Clouzot's first directorial effort, the mixture of comedy and mystery that we find in *L'Assassin habite au 21*, but also from most films of the Occupation. The film is relentless in its portrayal of the desire for power and authority, unforgiving in its unmasking of petty resentments and long-standing jealousies, and ruthless in its condemnation of corruption. How surprising then to find in this supreme expression of the depths of deceit and cowardice what one might call a light moment, what one might even consider a wink at the audience. When Denise leaves Germain's apartment after they have become lovers, after she has denounced his hypocrisy ('You're a coward, you're weak. Between the two of us, you're the tramp!'), we see ever so briefly a shadow just outside the door (Figure 16). The shape of the profile suggests Vorzet, but the shadow suggests a younger man, and the hat is not an accessory associated with Vorzet. It certainly isn't Denise or Germain. It is just a shadow, a reminder of the phantoms that haunt the most everyday places, and of the looks that surround us when we think no one is looking.

Notes

1 Michèle Lagny discusses the sense of voyeurism that pervades the film. See 'Les Français en focalisation interne', *Iris* 2.2 (1984), p. 95.

2 Vincendeau, Ginette, *Pépé le Moko* (London: British Film Institute, 1998).

3 Vincendeau, Ginette, 'French film noir in the classical era' in *European Film Noir*, edited by Andrew Spicer (Manchester: Manchester University Press, 2007), p. 30.

4 Chirat: *Le Cinéma français des années de guerre*, p. 110.

5 Ginette Leclerc described her screen persona as follows: 'My foremost speciality, as everyone knows, is vamps, easy women, and women of little virtue.' See Leclerc, Ginette, *Ma Vie privée* (Paris: Editions de la Table Ronde, 1963), p. 100. For discussions of Vichy propaganda featuring the ideal woman, see Pollard, Miranda, *Reign of Virtue: Mobilizing Women in Vichy France* (Chicago: University of Chicago Press, 1998), esp. ch. 2.

6 Mulvey's classic essay remains the most eloquent and concise statement of the connection between gender and point of view in the cinema. See Mulvey, Laura, 'Visual pleasure and narrative cinema', *Screen* 16.3 (Autumn 1975), pp. 6–18.

7 Burch and Sellier: *La Drôle de guerre des sexes du cinéma français 1930–1956*: p. 193

8 On the prevalence of anonymous letters of denunciation during the Occupation, see Halimi, André, *La Délation sous l'Occupation* (Paris: Alain Moreau, 1983). In his study of the town of Clermont-Ferrand during the Second World War, for example, John F. Sweets notes: 'The French police did not encourage anonymous denunciations, in part because the majority of such tips, upon investigation, were revealed to have originated in personal jealousies or commercial rivalries and seldom led the police to the discovery of serious criminal behaviour… The regional prefect spoke out against the practice… in February 1942 he ordered newspapers to publish a notice saying that anonymous denunciations were a serious offence and the perpetrators would be tracked down' (p. 23). See Sweets, John F., *Choices in Vichy France* (New York and Oxford: Oxford University Press, 1986).

9 All references to the different versions of the screenplay are drawn from the Archives Scénaristiques on *Le Corbeau* at the Bibliothèque du Film, Paris.

10 Noël Burch points out that the shift in Vorzet's role, from father to husband of Laura, makes the film far more reflective of typical themes of Vichy cinema, in particular, the 'criticism of the incestuous father and the idealization of women…'. See Burch and Sellier, *op. cit.*, p. 195.

11 A montage sequence is described in the final version of the screenplay (not present in the film), in which a series of scenes of the phenomenon of letter-writing makes clear that the poison pen letters have become part of the culture of the town. One man instructs his wife to write in capital letters; a young woman receives a bouquet of flowers with a note written in imitation of the

poison pen letters; a radio programme reports on all the strange places that the letters are appearing. At a village fair, a pickpocket retrieves an anonymous letter from a bystander's pocket; a carnival barker announces a fortune-teller by saying that she can see more than the poison pen letter-writer can. The letters even become prized possessions, with a collector offering to buy all the letters in existence.

12   Gregory Sims points out another change of emphasis from the original screenplays to the final film, the increasing importance of the couple Germain and Denise. In Sims's analysis, Denise's 'Dionysian instinctiveness' is what allows the transformation of Germain: '...through the formation of the couple of Germain and (the now pregnant) Denise, the film undeniably presents a clear sense of resolution, of *catharsis*, only not on the terrain of reason, but on the terrain of the instinctive, the sensual' (p. 772). I suggest that the only resolution the film offers is one of gender disorder. See Sims, Gregory, 'Henri-Georges Clouzot's *Le Corbeau* (1943): The work of art as will to power', *MLN (Modern Language Notes)* 11.4 (1999), pp. 743–779.

13   Included in the Archives Scénaristiques on *Le Corbeau* at the BIFI are articles by Locard on the Laval case, as well as a letter from Locard to Chavance accompanying one of the articles. Chavance's different versions of the screenplay are clearly indebted to Locard's work, and the designation of Laura as the culprit follows Locard's theories about anonymous letter-writing. In his essay on *Le Corbeau*, Gregory Sims (ibid.) describes the different versions of the screenplay and also notes Locard's influence on Chavance, as well as the ways in which Vorzet resembles Locard. But Sims makes one assertion for which I find no evidence in Locard's writings, namely that the guilty parties were 'often old maids suffering from sexual repression' (p. 768). The women suffer from sexual repression, to be sure, but Locard goes out of his way to describe Angèle Laval as an attractive, if thin, woman of 35. Sims regards the designation of Vorzet as the culprit in the film as a turning on its head of the stereotype of the '"scientific" logic of the repressed old maid' (p. 768). I would argue, rather, that the creation of Vorzet as the letter-writer has no source whatsoever in Locard's writings, and that Laura, as initially conceived, is the epitome of Locard's portrait of the anonymous letter-writer. The point is important in order to appreciate how thoroughly the designation of Vorzet as the villain in the final version of *Le Corbeau* departs from established opinion about *l'anonymographie*.

14   My summary of the *Affaire de Tulle* is drawn from these sources: Locard, Edmond, 'L'affaire de Tulle: Un cas typique d'anonymographie', *L'Avenir Médical* 20.7 (July–August 1923), pp. 3–7; Locard, Edmond, *Les Anonymographes* (Brussels: Ferdinand Larcier, 1923); Locard, Edmond, *La Vipère* (Paris: Editions de la flamme d'or, 1954); Locard, Edmond, *Mémoires d'un criminologiste* (Paris: Librairie Arthème Fayard, 1958); Camus, Michel, 'Angèle Laval', in *Les Grandes affaires criminelles*, vol. 9, edited by Roger Bernasconi (Geneva: Edito-Service

S.A., 1975), pp. 87–103. For a detailed account of the *Affair de Tulle* and its adaptation in *Le Corbeau*, see La Naour, Jean, *Le Corbeau: Histoire vraie d'une rumeur* (Paris: Hachette Littératures, 2006).

15 These characteristics of anonymous letter-writing are drawn from Locard: 'L'affaire de Tulle: un cas typique d'anonymographie', 3–7; and Locard: *Les Anonymographes.*

16 Burch and Sellier: *La Drôle de guerre des sexes du cinéma français 1930–1956*, p. 15.

17 Burch and Sellier: *La Drôle de guerre des sexes du cinéma français 1930–1956*, p. 192.

18 See, for example, Garçon, François, *De Blum à Pétain: cinéma et société française, 1936–1944* (Paris: Les Editions du Cerf, 1984), pp. 86–87; and Williams, Alan, *Republic of Images: A History of French Filmmaking* (Cambridge, MA, and London: Harvard University Press, 1992), pp. 260–261.

19 Francine Muel-Dreyfus, describing the effects of the legislation which implemented the death penalty for performing abortions, notes: 'The death penalty and the extreme penalties introduced by the law of February 15, 1942 affected women, some of whom belonged to the caring professions, and a single man about whom we know nothing. No doctor was sentenced. Poor and working-class women who lived in provincial towns where suspects were easily spotted were the easiest targets for accusation and conviction in this stage of the war against abortion, which was declared a crime against civil security.' See Muel-Dreyfus, Francine, *Vichy et l'éternel féminin* (Paris: Editions du Seuil, 1996), pp. 326–327.

3   Reception

Le Corbeau opened on 28 September 1943, at the Cinéma Normandie on the Champs-Elysées in Paris, the movie theatre where many Continental films had their premieres. The film was greeted with mostly laudatory reviews. Almost without exception, Clouzot is named in reviews as an enormously talented film director, and his particular gifts in the writing of dialogue and in masterfully directing scenes are emphasised. Given the various restrictions on the press that existed in France, and the attendant proliferation of collaborationist or fascist media outlets during the war, virtually all contemporary reviews of the film are less interesting as 'opinions' about the films in question and more interesting for their points of emphasis, or of elision. Put another way, film reviews in what was necessarily a collaborationist press are less interesting for what they actually 'say' about individual films than for what they either don't say or suggest in indirect ways.

In writing about *Le Corbeau*, many reviewers are writing about the Occupation, and the effect in reading some of these reviews is peculiar indeed. Despite the misgivings COIC might have had about the successful career of Henri-Georges Clouzot, *Le Film* was not about to criticise publicly a film by Continental. What is perhaps most interesting in the review that appeared in the journal, as in others of the time, is how the very subject of the film is addressed. Describing the film as a 'social and psychological drama' about a small town flooded with anonymous letters, the review states: '… this film unflinchingly portrays the ravages caused by the scourge: hidden sides of souls are revealed, dark tendencies kept hidden in everyday situations are released and accentuated. The unhealthy climate of this crisis is created on screen in a gripping way by H.-G. Clouzot…'[1] The reviewer seems to be talking about the war itself. The official reception of *Le Corbeau* thus offers the rare occasion to express discontent about the Occupation through the vehicle of the film.

Similarly, *Miroir de l'écran* (which also published a novelisation of the film) notes that the film treats 'one of the most repulsive stains on the human race: the anonymous letter. In this film made by Continental, the subject is developed with all of the vigor and the fierceness demanded by such actions.'[2] Again, one has the impression that the format of the film review, given the subject matter of this particular film, permits a commentary that goes far beyond the specific film (anonymous letters may well be repugnant, but to describe them as 'one of the most repulsive stains on the human race' reflects a fervour that situates the film in its time even more precisely than does the film itself). Jules Lhost, writing in *Cassandre*, provides yet another extremely intense reading of the film, in which he observes that a film like *Le Corbeau* 'must necessarily provoke a shock, a reaction, a start; it must open up a crack in a closed world and let us see the unknown aspects of the interior hell that everyone feeds on with constant and innocent ferociousness'.[3]

In sharp contrast to Lhost's and to most contemporary reviews of the film is the critique by François Vinneuil (the pseudonym of well-known fascist Lucien Rebatet, the author of the virulent anti-Semitic pamphlet *Les Tribus du cinéma et du théâtre*). Writing in the fascist and pro-German newspaper *Je Suis Partout* – which did its own considerable share of denunciations – Vinneuil is far more restrained than other critics in assessing the value of the film. If other critics seem to take the subject of the film as an opportunity to hold forth on the affront of anonymous letters, Vinneuil also seizes the opportunity to take the opposite stance, and to note the importance (yet also the banality) of anonymous letter-writing. Noting that anonymous letters are a relatively new subject for the cinema, Vinneuil says: 'The mystery and the scandalous attraction of the subject has dulled in recent years, since epistolary denunciations, death threats and insults (never signed), are among the daily essential routines of our gracious country, from Calais to Port-Vendres.' Hence, says Vinneuil, a journalist coming across a letter of the type that Germain receives in *Le Corbeau* could only shrug his shoulders and think nothing of it.[4]

While other reviewers seem to welcome the opportunity to describe the pathology of anonymous letter-writing, Vinneuil is quite circumspect. He writes, '[W]hen the anonymous letter takes on such determination and treachery, it becomes tragic.' Vinneuil carefully separates anonymous letter-writing in general from the specific case depicted in *Le Corbeau*. Vinneuil's overall opinion of the film is far more mixed than that of other reviewers. In what might be understood as a backhanded compliment, Vinneuil notes that the film holds one's interest and that 'during the 90 minutes of the film, the spectator isn't bored for one minute'. While Vinneuil notes Clouzot's gifts as a film-maker, he finds the director's approach to the subject of the film too facile, and ultimately he considers the film a disappointment.[5] Gregory Sims reads Vinneuil's review as that rare exception, a review that criticised *Le Corbeau* for not being dark enough.[6] One wonders, rather, if there is not a conceptual confusion in Vinneuil's review, the sense that when writing for a journal that itself embraced various forms of anonymous denunciation (addresses of Jews or resistants in hiding, for instance), the possibility of engaging fully with a film *about* anonymous letters is impossible.

Some reviews express a kind of bewilderment before the film, not just, or even necessarily because, the film is a masterpiece but because the experience of watching the film is unique. Roger Régent, writing in *Les Nouveaux Temps*, says that one cannot describe *Le Corbeau* in the same terms used to describe other films of the Occupation. Chavance and Clouzot, he says, 'through the plot and its visual presentation, succeed in holding the spectator in a state of suffocation that many will not be able to bear. Twenty times during the film, we feel the tip of the knife approaching our hearts: rarely has the cinema made us succumb to such tension.'[7] Audiberti, in the arts magazine *Comoedia*, reiterates Régent's observations by noting that the film 'proceeds with a skill that is nearly unbearable'. The author concludes on a curious note, stating explicitly what is more often implicit in other reviews of the film: 'The authors of *Le Corbeau* seem to have wanted to prove that if war is hard, peace isn't always peaceful. In any case, it is certain that all of

Le Corbeau's spectators will begin to send anonymous letters. Man is the devil.'[8]

Not all of these reviews, however, are uniformly positive, and *Le Corbeau* was controversial from the outset. Clouzot's brilliance as a film-maker paled for some critics in light of the unpleasant subject matter of the film. A critic for *Réveil* called the film *malsain* (unhealthy), but still praised the director, the writer and the actors.[9] More significantly, *Le Corbeau* was condemned by the Catholic Church. On a scale of 1 to 6, with '1' being a film for all audiences, even young children, and '6' being a film 'essentially pernicious in social, moral, or religious terms', *Le Corbeau* was one of the rare films to receive a '6' during the Occupation. The film was condemned as 'painful and hard, constantly morbid in its complexity'. Among the more specific complaints were premarital sex initiated crudely by a woman, a doctor whose intentions are unclear insofar as birth is concerned (interestingly, Dr Germain is not referred to in the Church's literature as an abortionist), a general atmosphere of suspicion extending even to a 14-year-old girl, a central and sympathetic character who is an atheist, as well as suicide, murder and foul language.[10]

Le Corbeau may have provoked mixed, and sometimes bizarre, reactions, but the film was a financial success. Yet according to Clouzot, he left Continental before the film premiered, in a split with Greven. Clouzot worked on various projects in the last months of 1943, including a collaboration with Jean-Paul Sartre on an adaptation of Vladimir Nabokov's novel *Camera Obscura* (the project was eventually abandoned). Clouzot also worked on two projects intended for actress Odette Joyeux, one of which was turned into a ballet, and the other of which was abandoned (according to the actress, the project was considered 'too dark' by producers).[11]

The decisive blow for *Le Corbeau*'s reputation – and its subsequent status, for better or worse, as the film of the Occupation – came in March 1944.[12] *Les Lettres Françaises* was a clandestine journal associated with the Resistance and published by the CNE (Comité National des Ecrivains, or National Writers' Committee), a group founded in May 1941 by anti-fascist intellectuals and writers. The first issue of *Les Lettres Françaises* appeared on 20 September 1942, and a total of 19 issues were published during the war.

Writers who published in the journal included Jean Guéhenno, Jean-Paul Sartre, Louis Aragon, Elsa Triolet, Paul Eluard and many others. Following both the philosophy and the format (six mimeographed pages) of *Les Lettres Françaises*, a similarly clandestine journal devoted to the cinema, *L'Ecran Français*, made its first appearance in December 1943. Initially affiliated with the cinema committees of the Front National (the Resistance group affiliated with the Communist Party), the organisation (and the journal) broadened in 1944 to include different film organisations associated with the Resistance. All of these groups together formed the organisation Comité de Libération du Cinéma Français (Committee for the Liberation of French Cinema). In issue number 14 (10 March 1944) of *Les Lettres Françaises*, it was announced on the front page that *L'Ecran Français* (as well as *La Scène Française*, devoted to the theatre) would be published in the pages of the literary journal.[13]

In that issue, Georges Adam and Pierre Blanchar co-authored an article entitled '*Le Corbeau* est déplumé' ('The Raven is Plucked') (since the journal was clandestine, the article was not signed at the time of its release). This is less a review of the film than a condemnation of it and, more importantly, it is a text that prepares the way for a settling of accounts insofar as the cinema and the Occupation are concerned. The essay is structured by a comparison between Clouzot's film and *Le Ciel est à vous*, a film by Jean Grémillon that came out in February 1944. Despite its focus on these two specific films, the very opening of the text signals its status as an overview of the cinema of the Occupation, that is, as a critical view that is signalling the end of the period in question. The authors state that no one can expect the cinema to be an arm of the Resistance in a period of Occupation, but that nonetheless there were choices available to film-makers. 'At the very least,' the authors write, 'we can ask the filmmaker to support the only language allowed by the circumstances that form the limits and the conditions of his current existence: the language of dignity, of internal greatness. Thus and only thus can he maintain his honor.'[14]

If such a demand seems unrealistic, the authors declare, one only has to look at the two films that characterise in bold terms the choices available to film-makers in France: *Le Corbeau* and *Le Ciel est à vous*. Adam and Blanchar condemn *Le Corbeau* for its portrait of the inhabitants of a French town as 'degenerates', and for its attempts to convince French spectators of 'our indignity and our urgent need to bow down to the whims and the morality of the virtuous Nazi'. The cinematic virtuosity on display in *Le Corbeau* is underscored by the authors as reinforcing the noxious qualities of the film ('The undeniable technical qualities of their work only make its despicable qualities all the more remarkable'). In contrast, *Le Ciel est à vous* is a film that saves the honour of French cinema. The authors of the essay offer a point-by-point comparison of the two films, beginning with the affirmation: 'To the deceitful, perverted and obscene girls of *Le Corbeau* created by Clouzot's enslaved mind, as if in direct response to a Nazi order, *Le Ciel est à vous* replies No! You're wrong! I'll show you what typical French people are about!'[15]

In the context of war, and of the brutal stakes of opposing forces, the essay seems first and foremost a text that uses the cinema only incidentally, and then as a vehicle to rouse French sentiment to recognise that the 'true' French spirit is one of heroism and loyalty, not of poison pen letters and deception. In the context of war, and more specifically in this case of the approaching end of the war, it is perhaps understandable that bold strokes of clear-cut opposition are strategically necessary in order to rally public opinion. Even with this context understood, the essay's strategic points are curious. For of all the films that could be cited to illustrate the notion of honour and dishonour, the authors chose two of the most ambiguous films made during the Occupation.

Obviously the point is to isolate Continental in general, Clouzot and *Le Corbeau* in particular, from the 'true' French cinema. In order to make such a distinction, the authors have not only to simplify both films – i.e., make one of them fascist and anti-French, the other resistant and truly French – but also eliminate anything that complicates these simple, straightforward messages. In the case of *Le Ciel est à vous*, the 'French values' argument comes up short indeed. The film does tell the story of a French married couple, and their desire to pursue their dream, aviation. In particular, the film tells the story of how a wife and mother learns to share her husband's passion for flight, which eventually leads her to break a world aviation record.

But the film is far more ambiguous about this French couple than Adam and Blanchar's essay would lead us to believe.[16] The couple have two children, a daughter and a son. The daughter's desires – to play the piano, to pursue a career in music instead of the pharmaceutical career selected by her mother – are quite literally sacrificed so that the parents, and particularly the mother, can pursue their own. The mother is offended when Jacqueline's piano teacher comes to pay a visit to the family to suggest that Jacqueline is gifted enough to pursue a musical career, and as punishment she forbids Jacqueline to play the piano at all (a new piano was purchased when the family garage business took off; the old piano was destroyed in the move). When the parents need money to pursue their dreams of aviation, they ask Jacqueline if she will agree to sell the piano, and, when the daughter says no, they sell it anyway.

Jacqueline's love of the piano is not a minor subplot in the film; rather, this thread of the film is central from the outset, and it is never resolved. Given that the music teacher is virtually the only townsperson who expresses support for the Gauthier family when Thérèse's plane is lost, the suggestion is made that the mother and father will soon come to realise that their daughter's dreams matter, too. But that suggestion is never really examined in the film itself, and one wonders if the film is far more ambivalent about women's desires than Thérèse's success would suggest.[17] The Adam and Blanchar essay is not concerned with positive or negative portrayals of women, but rather with how the couple are a vital portrayal of typical French people. Even so, the sacrifice of the child's dream on the altar of the parents' desire to fly is a central preoccupation of the film and necessarily complicates any notion of *Le Ciel est à vous* as an uncompromisingly glowing portrayal of the French family.

It is not surprising that an essay on the cinema in France in wartime, published in a clandestine Resistance journal, would not demonstrate particular interest in the ambiguities of particular films. But 'The Raven is Plucked' deliberately misreads the films in order to set up a black and white opposition. For instance, Thérèse, in Grémillon's film, is 'a young French mother who is strong and modest, who accomplishes all of her duties and whose heart is big enough to take on yet another heroic dream', and thus serves as a foil to Ginette Leclerc's Denise, who is, in the authors' words, a club-foot and a slut. François Vinneuil is described as being enthusiastic about *Le Corbeau* when in fact, as I have discussed earlier, he was far less enthusiastic than other critics. And *Le Corbeau* is described as a perfect example of Nazi oppression of the French, when according to most accounts the film was considered highly controversial by the Germans.[18]

The opposition between the two films may well make sense in a political tract, but nonetheless one cannot help noting that while Clouzot and Grémillon are contrasted as a collaborator and a resister (literally: Grémillon was a member of the Resistance), the isolation of *Le Corbeau* serves to make Clouzot the unique representative of Continental Films in general. There were certainly many film-makers, writers and actors one could name as well. True, Clouzot had a position of authority at Continental that others did not. But, by designating Clouzot and one particular film as the embodiments of collaboration, at least two tasks are accomplished.

First, one can blame one person rather than an entire group, including all of the people who worked for Continental. Hence this essay is the first step in the vilification of Clouzot immediately after the Second World War, taking attention away from the large group of people who worked for Continental. Second, by focusing on a particular film, the cinematic face of collaboration becomes an isolated example (by the same token, of course, the spirit of French pride the authors discern in *Le Ciel est à vous* could easily be taken as exceptional as well). The implication is that *most* French directors kept the spirit of France alive – but not Clouzot (and given that he wrote two films and directed yet another, his presence during the war is extensive enough to marginalise claims that he could not be an isolated example).

More to the point, it is important to ask why Clouzot and *Le Corbeau* *specifically* came under such attack. As accounts by actors suggest, Clouzot was not the most pleasant man to work for (see part 1), and this might have added to his already disagreeable reputation as a Continental employee who had benefited from the war to become a film author. If Clouzot himself was under attack, we cannot ignore the very focused anger directed at *Le Corbeau*. As I've suggested, *Le Corbeau* is a profoundly troubling film in terms of the gender anxieties it articulates, particularly insofar as the weakness of men and the power of women are concerned. For a Resistance determined to reaffirm the virility of France, a film that so threatened the stability of masculine identity was dangerous. If it seems a bit of a stretch to argue that gender politics entered into the controversy about Le Corbeau, then it's useful to remember the early stages of retribution against those who were perceived as enemies of France. In August 1944, just five months after the appearance of the condemnatory article, Paris was liberated, and the judgement of those who were perceived as having contributed to the subjugation of France began. The seeking out and punishment of real and imagined collaborators focused with particular rage on those women who were accused of 'horizontal collaboration', and whose heads were shaved in public rituals of scorn, humiliation and appalling festival-like atmospheres. Eventually the purges may well have moved to committee meetings and deliberations behind closed doors, but, from the very outset, the punishment of collaboration in France had very real gender ramifications.[19]

The cinema was one small part of the process of épuration (purification or purges) that gripped the country for well over a year, the effects of which were felt for many years later. While many individuals who contributed to the film industry during the Occupation were brought before committees and were eventually suspended or sent to prison, the purification of the cinema was far less dramatic than what occurred in other areas of culture. The most dramatic case of purification in the arts is that of intellectual Robert Brasillach, who was editor-in-chief of the virulent pro-Nazi newspaper Je Suis Partout as well as a novelist and an historian of the cinema (he co-authored Histoire du Cinéma, with Maurice Bardèche, which was published originally in 1935). Brasillach was tried for treason and was executed in February 1945.

Purges in the cinema began in September 1944, initially administered by the Resistance CLCF (Comité de libération du cinéma français, the Committee for the Liberation of French Cinema). At its meeting of 4 September, the CLCF made a list of eight film directors who would receive suspensions: Marcel Carné, André Cayatte, Henri-Georges Clouzot, Henri Decoin, Léo Joannon, D. Norman, Richard Pottier and Albert Valentin. Carné seems to have been on the list only because it had been announced in 1940 that he would direct for Continental (which he never did). All of the other directors, with the exception of D. Norman, were employed by Continental.[20] The official commissions for the purges were not established until mid-October, and curiously, at that time – just a month after the initial announcement of directors to be suspended – the CLCF provided names of actors to the commissions but not of directors.[21] It is odd, certainly, that the most obvious target for purification, a studio financed and run by the Nazis, would not receive immediate and vigorous punishment. Eventually, virtually every profession associated with the cinema was represented in the purges, from director, producer and actor to projectionist, make-up artist and usher. The entire process was chaotic at best, and produced many inconsistencies, like the make-up artist at Continental who was suspended from work, while some of the actors he prepared for the motion pictures received no punishment.[22]

All of the purges that took place after the liberation were affected by deep divisions within the Resistance between the Communist Party and Gaullists, divisions that concerned not only how collaborators would be punished but also how the 'new' France would be created and sustained. The case of the cinema was unique in one particular respect, however. COIC, as discussed in Chapter One, was created by Vichy, functioned as a collaborationist organisation, and was effectively controlled by the dictates of Greven and Continental Films. And yet, despite its origins, COIC remained in place after the Liberation as the organisation to assure the survival and success of the French film industry. Hence French film personnel who themselves had collaborated were in the position of deciding the fates of other film personnel.

The decision about Clouzot and *Le Corbeau* began on 17 October 1944, when a subcommittee of film directors of the CLCF agreed to the director's suspension. On 9 November, another meeting was held to prepare for a hearing on 29 November. The first order of business was *Le Corbeau*, and the primary case against the film was the infamous article from *L'Ecran Français*. Point by point, accusations against the film were considered: that the film was shown in Germany with the title *A Little French Town* (a false rumour first published in the journal *Candide* and later picked up by critics of the film); that the film was anti-French propaganda (the fact that Chavance's original screenplay was registered in 1937 made this claim somewhat weak). In his defence, Clouzot insisted that neither Greven nor Bauermeister (the director of production at Continental) wanted the film to be made, and that he saw the film as an opportunity to denounce the practice of anonymous letter-writing. The commission dismissed the charges against Le Corbeau, noting that 'the scenario existed before the creation of Continental and that Clouzot's desire to make the film against the wishes of Greven demonstrated that the director had no intention of making propaganda'.[23]

Bertin-Maghit asserts that, no matter how strong the case was against Le Corbeau, the film itself accounted for a very small part of the dossier compiled against Clouzot. Rather, says Bertin-Maghit, it was a range of activities on Clouzot's part that received the most sustained attention. First and foremost, Clouzot not only worked for Continental, as did other film directors, but by virtue of being in charge of the screenplay division, he was a 'company man', a house regular, far more invested in the Nazi firm's activities than other directors or writers. Clouzot's defence was that he received no offers from other film companies, and accepted the offer from Greven in order to be able to eat. Second, Clouzot was accused of being a Nazi sympathiser and of using the Hitlerian salute (as noted earlier, one cannot help but wonder if the visual gag in L'Assassin habite au 21 contributed to this perception). Clouzot admitted that he had some sympathies for National Socialism because of its anti-capitalist stance, but that he never acted in any capacity except in terms of what was best for the cinema. Others claimed in Clouzot's defence that he never spoke in pro-German terms, and a letter signed by 30 employees of Continental attested to this fact as well. That Clouzot facilitated the hiring of the Jewish screenwriter Jean-Paul Le Chanois was brought out as a factor in his favour.[24]

Third, Clouzot's associations with Greven but also with Suzy Delair, were cause for criticism and condemnation. An employee of Continental affirmed that Clouzot and Greven were close, and that they often socialised together. Suzy Delair was one of the stars of French cinema who made the infamous trip to Berlin in March 1942 – a group of film actors (many of whom, like Danielle Darrieux, later claimed they were coerced to make the trip) visited German film studios and attended the premiere of Premier Rendez-vous, the first (and only) French film shown in Germany during the war. Delair was known – accurately or not – as an enthusiastic proponent of collaboration. One of the stories most often circulated about Delair was that when the trip to Berlin was over, she complained to Greven that she was never officially presented to Dr Goebbels.

The commission concluded that

> Clouzot, as an important employee of Continental, is truly a man of the company, he carefully defended its interests, and it is very difficult to believe that a man who did not have pro-German sentiments would have such close and intimate relations with a woman who, like Mlle Delair, displayed her sentiments so clearly and ostentatiously.[25]

Clouzot received a suspension, and his case went through several levels of judgement and appeal (the cases of film directors who received the punishment of suspension were reviewed either automatically or at the request of the film-maker). Interestingly, Suzy Delair – so influential in the original consideration of Clouzot's case – received initially only a three-month suspension.[26]

Screenings of *Le Corbeau* were prohibited in France, along with *Les Inconnus dans la maison* (scripted by Clouzot) and *La Vie de plaisir* (directed by Albert Valentin).[27] These three Continental films were considered, in one way or another, anti-French propaganda. The virulence surrounding *Le Corbeau* made it the most obvious candidate for censorship. *La Vie de plaisir* (which appeared in May 1944 and was therefore a fresh reminder of Continental) is a biting social satire in which wealthy families and the Church are presented as corrupt (the film seems more likely to have offended Vichy than the CLCF, but on more than one occasion the 'moral values' of the Right and the Resistance values of the Left coincided in agreement). The choice of *Les Inconnus dans la maison* is a bit puzzling; one assumes that Raimu's famous speech in the courtroom, denouncing the bourgeoisie of the French town, was seen as yet another denunciation of the French. In any case, the inclusion of *Les Inconnus dans la maison* made the denunciation of Clouzot even stronger.

In the pages of *Les Lettres Françaises* and *Le Film Français* (which become the official organ of the French film industry in 1944, replacing *Le Film*, the official Vichy film journal during the war), arguments about the politics of

Le Corbeau continued. In January 1945, the last film made by Continental (but unfinished at the end of the war), *Les Caves du Majestic* (directed by Richard Pottier and based on a novel by Georges Simenon), was completed and released. In response to the release of the film, an article in *Les Lettres Françaises*, 'Must *Le Corbeau* be authorized?', once again took aim at Clouzot's film. As if anticipating the objection that *Le Corbeau* is a work of cinematic art, the author claims that the film is not as good as others have claimed, and in any case that even if it wasn't shown in Germany, as had been claimed, it still was profoundly anti-French. Because *Les Caves du Majestic* is not a very good film, the article states, it is acceptable for it to be shown, even if it was made by Continental, whereas *Le Corbeau* should not be seen. Noting that the 'darkness' of *Le Corbeau* evokes other pessimistic works of art (like Stroheim's *The Wedding March*, 1928, and Zola's novel *La Bête humaine*), the fact that the film was financed by the Nazis is again the decisive factor. The bottom line, thus, is the presumed 'anti-French' quality of the film, which no discussion of pessimism or artistic value can modify.[28]

Louis Chavance defended the film in the pages of *Les Lettres Françaises* and *Spectateur*, and noted in particular how even though he and Clouzot had not been accused of any wrongdoing in terms of the film (Clouzot was suspended for his activities, not for this particular film), new rumours were circulating.[29] In particular, the nasty rumour that the film had been shown in Germany as a propaganda tool, with the title 'A Little French Town', refused to die (the story was invented as part of the ongoing effort to incriminate the film). The Communist film historian Georges Sadoul, who was one of the most virulent critics of *Le Corbeau*, responded to Chavance, and in particular to the distribution of the film during the war. In a peculiarly blindsided acknowledgement that the film was never distributed in Germany (as Sadoul himself had claimed), the author says that it was shown in Czechoslovakia and Romania during the war – that is, in countries predisposed to friendship with France, yet occupied by Hitler – and that is even worse than if the film had been shown in Germany! (There is no indication that this claim was true.)[30]

On 28 May 1946, two commissions differed in their proposals concerning Clouzot, with one recommending a six-month suspension while the other recommended a suspension of two years. This time *Le Corbeau* was an important factor in deciding Clouzot's fate.[31] Given that other directors who worked at Continental were either not punished or given very short suspensions, the reminder of the controversy provoked by *Le Corbeau* was a way of ensuring that Clouzot would be singled out for harsh punishment. The decision to maintain Clouzot's suspension for two additional years provoked angry responses from those who insisted that Clouzot be able to continue to work and that *Le Corbeau* be screened. *Les Temps Modernes*, the influential journal affiliated with Jean-Paul Sartre and Simone de Beauvoir, published an editorial in its first issue, in which the administration of the sanctions was called into account. Noting the 'Kafkaesque' (a word used more than once to described the situation in the cinema in general and vis-à-vis *Le Corbeau* in particular) quality of the process, the editors observe with considerable irony the fact that former members of COIC were judging the collaborationist activities of others. The ongoing nature of the punishment – with sanctions that continue until the next review, instead of a definitive sentence – smacks of a failure to assume or accept responsibility. Those who have been charged, the editors say, live in a constant state of waiting, of not knowing if or for how long they are to be punished.[32]

In the pages of the left-wing *Combat* (a newspaper that arose in clandestinity) on 4 October 1946, several film-makers defended the film and the director, calling *Le Corbeau* a 'quality film' (Autant-Lara) that should be judged in artistic terms (Marcel L'Herbier). Marcel Carné notes that those who banned the film were too dense to realise that their actions only intensify the public's desire to see the film. Interestingly, in these responses we see the 'aesthetic' defence of the film – that is, the need and desire to separate whatever controversies it might have inspired from its qualities as a work of film art. One suspects that given the climate and the sustained attacks on the film, an actual defence of the film on its own terms – that is, as a film very much preoccupied with 'darkness' not just in aesthetic terms but in terms of human desires and motivations – was not considered advantageous.[33]

Clouzot and Chavance were not the only individuals associated with *Le Corbeau* who were punished. Pierre Fresnay starred in four films produced by Continental, which made him something of a 'man of the house' as well, but the main reason for his arrest in September 1944 was his service in the actors' organisation established by Vichy. Fresnay spent six weeks in prison and was released.[34] His first film after the liberation was *La Fille du diable* (1946), directed by Henri Decoin. Ginette Leclerc was also arrested. She thought the main reason for her arrest was her appearance in three Continental films (*Val d'enfer/The Valley of Hell* and *Le Dernier sou/The Last Penny* [the latter not released until 1946], as well as *Le Corbeau*). But Leclerc also owned a cabaret (operated by her husband, the actor Lucien Gallas) and she was able to obtain the required papers for the cabaret to operate because of the intervention of Greven. There was also a vague rumour that Leclerc was guilty of 'horizontal collaboration' because of a photograph that circulated of her with a German soldier. Leclerc spent a year in prison, and first appeared in films again in 1947.[35] Almost the entire supporting cast of the film received some kind of sanction, ranging from 'blame' (Liliane Maigné [Rolande] and Pierre Bertin [the Assistant-Prefect]) to suspensions lasting anywhere from three months (Jean Brochard [Bonnevi] and Louis Seigner [Dr Bertrand]) to a year (Micheline Francey [Laura]). Antoine Balpêtré (Dr Delorme) was imprisoned. As Raymond Chirat emphasises, most of these actors performed other activities, such as radio broadcasts, considered collaborationist.[36] The fact remains, nonetheless, that *Le Corbeau* was highly visible as the embodiment of collaboration, punishment and retribution in the cinema.

For some peculiar reason, even after Clouzot's suspension for two years was affirmed in 1946, he was able to return to film-making in February 1947, when he began work on *Quai des Orfèvres*. Is this a case of a heavily taxed bureaucratic system in which one regulatory commission was not aware of what another was doing? Or, in Pierre Billard's words, of how, in the disorder of the era, 'Kafka could play against *The Castle*'?[37] Perhaps the strong emotions of the immediate post-war era had played themselves out, and perhaps some in the film industry recognised that French cinema was better off with Clouzot as a part of it rather than as its pariah. Marcel Carné was correct in his assessment that those who condemned and censored the film made the public more eager to see it, for *Le Corbeau* was shown 'unofficially' in numerous venues. According to Roland Lacourbe, any film-maker visiting France in the years immediately following the end of the war had two requests: a screening of *Le Corbeau* (in the basement of the American embassy) and a meeting with Clouzot.[38] The film was also shown clandestinely in ciné-clubs and various other 'unauthorised' venues. When Clouzot won the Best Director award (for *Quai des Orfèvres* at the Venice Film Festival in 1947), it became apparent that the continued censorship of *Le Corbeau* was not only unnecessary but irrelevant. The film was shown again in September, 1947, just a month before the release of *Quai des Orfèvres*.

Two of the most interesting responses to *Le Corbeau* and the scandal surrounding it emerged in 1947 and 1948, responses that were close to the Liberation period but that attempted to take stock of why the film had been so controversial. In 1947, *Le Monde illustré théâtral et littéraire* published the screenplay for the film, with an afterword by Lo Duca (this was the first time the journal published a film screenplay, thus suggesting the status that the film had acquired).[39] Duca takes a cynical view of the re-release of *Le Corbeau* in 1947, since, he says, those who wanted to see the film managed to see it during the several years of its disappearance from public view through 'unofficial' screenings, and its official re-emergence was simply a way to make money – that is, to put aside scandal and controversy when financial gain was to be had. Picking up on a theme that was suggested by previous defenders of the film as well as by Louis Chavance, Duca describes *Le Corbeau* as a 'revolutionary film' that provided an uncomfortable – and, after the Liberation, an unwelcome – reminder that anonymous letter-writing was rampant during the Occupation. Ultimately, says Luca, particularly given the fact that many of those who worked for Continental not only received no punishment but were treated as patriots after the war, the controversy about *Le Corbeau* was really about the talents of Clouzot.[40] If some defenders of *Le Corbeau* attempted to praise the aesthetic quality of the film and leave out the politics, Duca insists upon the vision of the film as aesthetic and political at the same time:

> *Le Corbeau* spares no one. It mercilessly shows the fragility of the individual conscience, the baseness of the collective conscience, and the rarity of a sound thought or a free man. It dares to show an elementary truth: the dualism that dominates every human being, the black and white sides of every soul, the objective sadness of the monster seated next to the angel, that 'Hitler in uns selbst' (Hitler is within us all) of which Max Picard spoke.[41]

Lo Duca's comments on the film and its significance did not signal an end to the controversy about the film. They do suggest that the simplistic dichotomy of a resistant versus a collaborationist film, or, for that matter, an 'immoral' versus a 'well-made' film, was visibly and publicly open to challenge and criticism.

In 1948, Roger Régent published the first book-length reflection on French cinema of the Occupation, *Cinéma de France: De la fille du puisatier aux enfants du paradis*. Régent had been a film critic during the war, and his goal in the book was to take stock of the accomplishments of French film-makers during the Occupation, year by year, from 1940 to 1944. With the hindsight of a few years, Régent describes *Le Corbeau* as an 'incomparable work... with its icy violence, its corrosive power over the spectator...'. 'This film', claims Régent, 'will remain the most brutal cinematic sensation of these four years.'[42] Although Régent's stated goal in his book is to 'avoid any political interference', he acknowledges that the controversy over *Le Corbeau* so affected its reception that it is impossible *not* to discuss it.[43] Like Duca, Régent argues that the anger over *Le Corbeau* was directed at Clouzot's talent ('one couldn't forgive Henri-Georges Clouzot for his talent'). Régent is predictably critical of the condemnation of the film, and he raises an interesting question that anticipates how French cinema made during the war will be seen by the rest of the world: 'It is unfortunate that French cinema was the battleground for such manoeuvres [i.e., the attacks on *Le Corbeau*], and that their justification was propaganda and national honour. Can we be sure that the spectacle of such operations isn't as serious for the prestige of France as a story – even under enemy Occupation, even told with talent – about anonymous letters?'[44]

Le Corbeau was shown outside of France in 1948, and in England and the US, it premiered after *Quai des Orfèvres*. Reviews in both *The New York Times* and *The Times* suggest that *Le Corbeau* would for ever – or at least, in 1948 – be associated with controversy. Bosley Crowther, writing for *The New York Times*, seems to sympathise with those who condemned the film: '... however the [French] Government may now view it, it cannot be denied that *Le Corbeau* puts a black complexion upon the character of the petit-bourgeois French. In fact, it paints a thoroughly grim picture of the questionable nature of mankind. And if this isn't intentionally discouraging, it doesn't help to raise the spirits a bit.'[45] The reviewer for *The Times* says that most of the film's characters are 'worthless enough to deserve most of the scurrilous things "the crow" writes about them …'. In general, the reviewer concludes, '*Le Corbeau* does not add to the considerable reputation of its director'.[46] In very different ways, film reviewers and filmgoers in the post-war years in Britain and the US were responding to the war and to the French, and reactions to Clouzot's film, only a few short years after the end of the Second World War, are necessarily defined by an attempt to come to terms with France's initial defeat, occupation by Germany and eventual liberation. Naturally reviewers can simply not like a given film, but these reviews suggest that the emergence of French films made during the Occupation on an international level – and especially, perhaps, a film as provocative as *Le Corbeau* – would require some time to accommodate.

Eventually, *Le Corbeau* would become considered a classic of the French cinema. One of the popular indications of the status of the film occurred in 1950, when *Cinémonde*, one of the most popular film magazines in France, published an issue in its series 'Le Film Vécu' ('Real-Life Film') devoted to Pierre Fresnay and *Le Corbeau*. The premise of the series was the retelling of a film from the point of view of the actor's character. The issue includes an overview of Fresnay's career, an article by him on his approach to acting, and a 'first-person' version of *Le Corbeau* (its opening lines are: 'Why did I flee blindly … did the ghosts that pursued me stop, like an arrow reaching its target, in Saint-Robin? I don't know'). The focus of the issue may well be Fresnay, but its cover features Fresnay in close-up with the title: '*Le Corbeau*, le grand film de Pierre Fresnay.'[47] The writings by Lo Duca and Roger Régent were important in terms of how individuals in the world of arts and letters were accounting for the status of *Le Corbeau* and the scandal surrounding it; the issue of *Cinémonde* affirms that *Le Corbeau* had re-entered popular cinema culture in France.

The fact that Clouzot kept on making films accounted for some changes in how *Le Corbeau* would be understood, since it was now part of what was becoming a distinguished (if always a bit difficult to classify) cinematic career. It does not require too much imagination to see in the first films

Clouzot made after his return to film-making – *Quai des Orfèvres*, but especially *Manon* (1949) – a settling of scores. The producer who financed Clouzot's return to film-making with *Quai des Orfèvres* insisted that the film not be too 'dark'. Clouzot returned – somewhat perversely, one cannot help but think – to the formula that he perfected at Continental in the early years of the Occupation: a mystery once again based upon a novel by Stanislas Steeman (and to which the author once again objected), with considerable twists, including a music-hall storyline. Suzy Delair starred in the film, not as Mila Malou (there was no detective Wens in the story) but as Jenny Lamour, an excitable and ambitious performer very much in the mould of her previous roles in *Le Dernier des six* and *L'Assassin habite au 21*. Perhaps most provocatively, in this film, which would supposedly demonstrate Clouzot's 'respectability' as a film director, he created the character (not present in the novel) of a lesbian photographer.[48] If *Quai des Orfèvres* marked the return of the director to the French film industry, attempting to rebuild and re-imagine itself after the war, Clouzot made certain to provide provocative representations of desire, deceit and deception. Most important in terms of the rehabilitation of Clouzot's career, the film was enormously popular.

Clouzot's next feature film, *Manon*, is a very explicit settling of accounts. An updated version of Abbé Prévost's classic 1731 novel *Manon Lescaut*, the film is set during the Liberation and its aftermath. The central character, Manon, is a young woman in a small town about to become a victim of the 'wild purges' because of rumours about her activities during the war. She is saved by Desgrieux, a member of the Resistance FFI (Forces Françaises de l'Intérieur), and they go to Paris, where they discover a corrupt world ruled by black marketeering. Manon, unbeknownst to Desgrieux, begins working as a prostitute, and when he learns this he becomes a drug addict and commits murder. The couple flee to Marseille, where they board a ship for Palestine. Once there, they become embroiled in a conflict between Israelis and Arabs, and Manon dies in Desgrieux's arms. Predictably, perhaps, Clouzot's film met with appalled reviews, but they had more to do with his depiction of 'human nature' than of the post-war period per se.[49] (Like *Quai des Orfèvres* before it, *Manon* received a prize at the Venice Film Festival). Clouzot also contributed to a 'sketch' film about the return of prisoners and concentration camp survivors to France (one of the other contributors was Clouzot's former colleague at Continental, André Cayatte), *Retour à la vie*, in 1949.

Between 1947 and 1950, Clouzot directed three features (as well as his contribution to *Retour à la vie*), the busiest period of his career. (The third film, after *Quai des Orfèvres* and *Manon*, is a period piece, *Miquette et sa mère*, which even the most ardent supporters of Clouzot's work found trivial.) In the 1950s, Clouzot did not really fit in either of the categories that have become convenient shorthand for the era, for he was not a part of the 'tradition of quality', nor was he considered, along with Jacques Becker, Jacques Tati and Robert Bresson, for example, a part of the *auteur* cinema. Like the directors associated with the tradition of quality, Clouzot adapted literary works to the screen, but they were mystery and detective novels, not classics of French literature. He certainly had a distinctive style – any discussion of film noir in French cinema would be incomplete without consideration of Clouzot's work, for instance – but whether it was because of his controversial past in the Second World War or because of personal disagreements, Clouzot never received the approval of the critics of *Cahiers du Cinéma* as they emerged as major arbiters of cinematic innovation in the 1950s.

Clouzot's best-known works, aside from *Le Corbeau*, are *Le Salaire de la peur/The Wages of Fear* (1953) and *Les Diaboliques* (1955). Both films are masterpieces of suspense, and both were adaptations of popular novels by Georges Arnaud and the writing duo of Pierre Boileau and Thomas Narcejac, respectively. But despite the critical and commercial success of these films, Clouzot has always been more recognised for the success of particular films than for his entire career. He did not make a large number of films – ten feature films in all, in addition to his contribution to *Retour à la vie* and his documentary about Picasso, *Le Mystère Picasso/The Mystery of Picasso* (1956). After the Picasso film, Clouzot's last three features (*Les Espions* (*Spies*) [1957]; *La Vérité* (*Truth*) [1960]; and *La Prisonnière* (*The Prisoner*) [1968], never brought him the acclaim of his earlier films. And in any case, Clouzot's later films seemed less engaged in the provocative exploration of human desires and the visual exploration of darkness and shadows than his earlier work (despite the fact that his last film, *The Prisoner*, explores sadomasochism and the presumed desires of women).

Clouzot's career never escaped the shadow of the scandal of *Le Corbeau*. Although some of Clouzot's films have achieved the status of classics, including *Quai des Orfèvres*, *Les Diaboliques* and *Le Salaire de la peur*, none of these films (with the possible exception of *Quai des Orfèvres*, which is situated in a post-war era) is as attached to a specific time and place as is *Le Corbeau*. Indeed, Clouzot's film remains to this day the emblematic film of the German Occupation of France. How, then, has the film emerged in accounts of the period? General historical accounts of the Second World War and France may have the occasional reference to the film and the uproar it caused, as well as to Continental Films as an example of German control of culture, but, not surprisingly, it is in the accounts of film critics and historians devoted to the period that we find sustained discussion of the film. In a special 1973 issue of *Les Cahiers de la Cinémathèque* devoted to the cinema of Vichy, Marcel Oms takes a fresh look at *Le Corbeau* and the controversy it unleashed. Noting that Georges Sadoul never retreated from his condemnation of the film (in 1954, Sadoul wrote in *Le Cinéma pendant la guerre* that much of the anger directed at *Le Corbeau* was outrage that French citizens could be shown as so susceptible to the spell of anonymous letter-writing), Oms points out the obvious – that French citizens did write anonymous letters and that the Resistance was well aware of the fact. In affirming that 'Today, definitively, *Le Corbeau* occupies its place in history', Oms sees the film as crucial to our comprehension not just of an era but of how an era is understood.[50]

In 1981, Jacques Siclier's *La France de Pétain et son cinéma* explored in depth the cinema of the Occupation from the point of view of an impassioned spectator (Siclier recounts his own experiences as a movie-viewer during the war). *Le Corbeau* receives extensive attention in Siclier's account as one of the masterpieces of cinema of the Occupation. While Siclier acknowledges the various compromises and accommodations made by French film-makers during the war, he nonetheless praises those film-makers for keeping French cinema alive, for refusing to make propaganda for the Germans, and for maintaining a level of cinematic excellence.[51]

The first full-length studies of French cinema and the Occupation, aside from Régent's 1948 book, were published in the early to mid-1980s, including works by Jean-Pierre Bertin-Maghit, Raymond Chirat, François Garçon and

Jean-Pierre Jeancolas.[52] Particularly influential is the first (and to date the only) English-language study of the period, published in 1985 by Evelyn Ehrlich. Although she emphasises from the outset that her book is not intended to provide critical analyses of individual films (p. xii), her discussion of *Le Corbeau* remains one of the most complete and influential.[53] Echoing the same spirit articulated by Lo Duca in 1947, Ehrlich argues that 'it was not simply Clouzot's and Chavance's attacks on French hypocrisy which so angered the Left. Rather, the underlying problem was their world-view, their refusal to acknowledge that moral positions were clear-cut.'[54] The title of Ehrlich's book – *Cinema of Paradox* – has remained the most influential description of French Occupation cinema, and *Le Corbeau* the most succinct expression of that paradox, a film made by a Nazi company in an occupied country that gloriously refuses to see the world in terms of moral absolutes.

As influential as Ehrlich's analysis has been, some discussions of the film in more recent years have challenged its status as 'paradoxical'. Noël Burch and Geneviève Sellier, in their historically rich analysis of the representation of gender in French cinema, consider *Le Corbeau* to be venomous in its portrayal of the French populace and reflective of the right-wing anarchism presumably espoused by Clouzot.[55] A series of essays by Gregory Sims, including one on *Le Corbeau*, has challenged virtually every critical truism about the determination of French film-makers to keep French cinema 'French' and untainted by Nazi influence. Sims sees *Le Corbeau* as far from paradoxical, but rather as an affirmation, through the journey of Dr Germain, of one man's engagement with the world in terms consonant with the fascist ideology of the era.[56]

If the study of French cinema during the Occupation was once a barely explored terrain, more and more studies have appeared in recent years, including rich and detailed historical studies by Jean-Louis Bertin-Maghit.[57] The particular significance of Clouzot's film has tended to recede in favour of an approach that takes a longer view (and hence one less attuned to the qualities of specific films) on cinema of the Occupation. There is no question, however, that *Le Corbeau* will likely remain through different interpretative grids and different historical emphases as the emblematic film of the Occupation.

Le Corbeau has been remade once, in a 1951 film, The 13th Letter, directed by Otto Preminger. The outlines of the story remain the same, but the setting is switched to a small town in French-speaking Canada. Dr Germain becomes Dr Pearson (Michael Rennie), recently arrived from London, where he had a successful gynaecological practice. We gradually learn that his wife left him, then begged him for a reconciliation, and then killed herself after he refused. Dr Vorzet becomes Dr Laurent (Charles Boyer), married to Cora (Constance Smith), many years his junior. Some scenes from Le Corbeau are imitated very closely in Preminger's film, while there are many omissions from Clouzot's and Chavance's screenplay (and, interestingly, only Chavance gets screenplay credit). There is no mention of abortion and no pregnancy, and there is no mention of drugs. The two women who are so sharply contrasted in Le Corbeau, Laura and Denise (now Cora and Denise), are here very similar in appearance (both women are brunette and conventionally attractive; Denise is played by Linda Darnell), except for Denise's limp. If there is the suggestion of an initial distinction between them (Cora, the seemingly reputable doctor's wife; Denise, who is, as in Clouzot's film, introduced in bed), it quickly becomes apparent that Cora is troubled and that Denise is an appropriate love object. Rochelle (Rolande) and Marie Corbin are still busybodies, and initial suspicion falls once again on Marie Corbin. Some of the important scenes in Le Corbeau, including the funeral procession, the letter falling from the church balcony, and the dictation session, are re-enacted in the film.[58]

The 13th Letter is not considered one of Preminger's finest works, but the film is interesting as a bridge between a French and American film noir. While a small town in Canada is certainly not the typical setting for an American film noir, Preminger succeeds in creating an atmosphere of claustrophobia and paranoia. A large portrait of Cora, with a somewhat devilish smile, hangs in the office of Dr Laurent, surely reminding the viewer of the portrait of Laura in Preminger's best-known film noir, Laura (1944). It is difficult, as is so often the case with remakes, not to see the film as inferior to Le Corbeau. But two particular aspects of the film suggest what is at stake in the adaptation of a French film noir for an American audience. First, one of the working oppositions in the film is between those who speak with a French accent and those who don't! That the poison pen writer is not a native speaker of English is apparent with the first several letters, some of which are written in stilted English ('Dr Pearson, before I tell Dr Laurent about you and Cora, I give you this chance to leave town').

The most interesting ramification of this French/English distinction concerns the 'cancer patient' (here, Jean-Louis Gautier, a war hero who does not have cancer but is told so in a letter) and his mother. The casting of Sylvie in Clouzot's film gives the mother's revenge a particular contour of divine retribution. The veteran French actress Françoise Rosay plays Mme Gautier, Preminger's version of the mother of the cancer victim in *Le Corbeau*. Like Dr Laurent, Mme Gautier speaks English with an accent, so that the web of possible suspects includes her. Yet her presence – robust, blonde and very assertive – provides a counterpoint to Dr Laurent in terms of the peculiar way in which the film presents a town separated by accents: she is the strong mother, Dr Laurent is the weak husband. When Mme Gautier and Dr Pearson speak (here, it is during the dictation session, not afterwards), the woman's resolve is apparent and Pearson's apprehension is palpable. As she leaves the room where they are speaking, she looks into the room where the dictation session occurs, through the frosted glass of a door, with only her eyes visible through the etched lettering. The effect is stunning in a film that all too often seems like a somewhat mechanical exercise in adaptation.

It is, of course, common to say that one's favourite films, or those one judges particularly important, could never be remade. In the case of *Le Corbeau*, this isn't just a matter of aesthetic quality. For *Le Corbeau* is a film that can never really be understood outside of a specific historical situation, one shaped by polarisation, by compromise, by deceit. Of course all viewers, whether familiar with the German occupation of France or not, will read *Le Corbeau* in particular ways that may well have nothing to do with its immediate historical context, or rather, may have more to do with a different, related context than the one that produced the film. The magnitude of the film's achievement, however, is all the more remarkable when we consider that debates about its relationship to fascism, collaboration and authority are still ongoing.

Notes

1   NA, 'Review of *Le Corbeau*', *Le Film* 74 (9 October 1943), p. 12.

2   Muhrer, Luc, '*Le Corbeau*', *Miroir de l'Ecran* (25 October 1943), p. 18.

3   Lhost, Jules, 'Review of *Le Corbeau*', *Cassandre* (12 December 1943), p. 16.

4   Vinneuil, François, 'Lettres anonymes', *Je Suis Partout* (8 October 1943), p. 7.

5   Vinneuil, François, 'Lettres anonymes', *Je Suis Partout* (8 October 1943), p. 7.

6   Sims: 'Henri-Georges Clouzot's *Le Corbeau* (1943): the work of art as will to power', p. 760.

7   Régent, Roger, 'Review of *Le Corbeau*', *Les Nouveaux Temps* (9 October 1943).

8   Audiberti, 'Review of *Le Corbeau*', *Comoedia* (9 October 1943), p. 26.

9   Cited in Bocquet and Godin: *Clouzot Cinéaste*, p. 37.

10   Siclier: *La France de Pétain et son cinéma*, p. 453.

11   Bocquet and Godin: *Clouzot Cinéaste*, pp. 32–33.

12   For a discussion of the controversy provoked by *Le Corbeau*, see Schwengler, Olivier, '*Le Corbeau*', *CinémAction* 103 (2002), pp. 44–50. The issue is devoted to '50 films that provoked scandals'.

13   Barrot, Olivier, *L'Ecran français, 1943–1953: Histoire d'un journal et d'une époque* (Paris: Les éditeurs français réunis, 1979), pp. 11–13.

14   Barrot: *L'Ecran français, 1943–1953: Histoire d'un journal et d'une époque*, p. 14. The entire text of the Blanchar and Adam article is reprinted in Barrot's book.

15   Barrot: *L'Ecran français, 1943–1953: Histoire d'un journal et d'une époque*, p. 14.

16   For a discussion of different responses to the film, see Semple, Jeanie, 'Ambiguities in the film *Le Ciel est à vous*', in *Vichy France and the Resistance: Culture and Ideology*, edited by Roderick Kedward and Roger Austin (London and Sydney: Croom Helm, 1985), pp. 123–132.

17   Geneviève Sellier argues that Jacqueline's desires for a musical career embody in the film the contradiction experienced by a mother who wants to pursue her own desires. See Burch and Sellier: *La Drôle de guerre des sexes du cinéma français 1930–1956*, p. 200.

18   Barrot: *L'Ecran français, 1943–1953: Histoire d'un journal et d'une époque*, pp. 14–15.

19   See Virgili, Fabrice, *La France 'virile': Des femmes tondues à la libération* (Paris: Editions Payot et Rivages, 2000; rpt. 2004).

20   Bertin-Maghit: *Le Cinéma français sous l'Occupation* (Paris: Perrin, 1989; rpt. 2002), p. 194, p. 317n.

21   Bertin-Maghit: *Le Cinéma français sous l'Occupation* (Paris: Perrin, 1989; rpt. 2002), pp. 204–205.

22   Bertin-Maghit: *Le Cinéma français sous l'Occupation* (Paris: Perrin, 1989; rpt. 2002), p. 214.

23   Bertin-Maghit: *Le Cinéma français sous l'Occupation* (Paris: Perrin, 1989; rpt. 2002), p. 225.

24   Bertin-Maghit: *Le Cinéma français sous l'Occupation* (Paris: Perrin, 1989; rpt. 2002), pp. 224–226.

25   Bertin-Maghit: *Le Cinéma français sous l'Occupation* (Paris: Perrin, 1989; rpt. 2002), pp. 226–227.

26   Bertin-Maghit: *Le Cinéma français sous l'Occupation* (Paris: Perrin, 1989; rpt. 2002), p. 438. In a 1999 interview, Delair responded to a question about her memories of the Occupation and liberation: 'We [she & Clouzot] had a very difficult time. We were judged many times. But everything was false.' See Le Bellego, Gaël, 'Avec... Madame Suzy Delair', *L'Avant-Scène Cinéma* 487 (December 1999), p. 77.

27   The announcement that these three films (as well as all films by Sacha Guitry) would continue to be prohibited was announced in *Le Film Français*. See NA, 'Des Films 'Continental' *Le Corbeau, Les Inconnus dans la maison, La Vie de plaisir*, et les films de Guitry restent interdits', *Le Film Français* 15 (16 March 1945), p. 7.

28   NA, 'Faut-Il autoriser *Le Corbeau?*', *Les Lettres Françaises* (1 December 1945).

29   Chavance, Louis, 'Sur *Le Corbeau*', *Spectateur* (10 April 1946); Chavance, Louis, 'Point final', *Les Lettres Françaises* (3 May 1946).

30   Sadoul, Georges, '*Le Corbeau*', *Les Lettres Françaises* (3 May 1946).

31   Bertin-Maghit: *Le Cinéma français sous l'Occupation*, (Paris: Perrin, 1989; rpt. 2002) p. 227.

32   NA, 'A La Kafka', *Les Temps Modernes* 1 (October–November 1945).

33   *Combat* (4 October 1946). Reprinted in Louis Chavance and Henri-Georges Clouzot, *Le Corbeau* (Paris: La Nouvelle Edition, 1948), pp. 220–222.

34   Dubeux, Albert, *Pierre Fresnay* (Paris: Calmann-Lévy, 1950), pp. 86–87.

35   Gilles, Christian, *Ginette Leclerc: Le désir des hommes* (Paris: L'Harmattan, 2000), pp. 17–19.

36   Chirat: *Le Cinéma français des années de guerre*, p. 117.

37   Billard: *L'Age classique du cinéma français: Du cinéma parlant à la Nouvelle Vague*, p. 472.

38   Lacourbe, Roland, *Henri-Georges Clouzot* (Paris: L'Avant-scène Cinéma, 1977, series *Anthologie du Cinéma* no. 94), p. 98; reprinted from *L'Avant-scène Cinema* 186 (15 April 1977).

39   Chavance, Louis, and Henri-Georges Clouzot, *Le Corbeau* (Paris: Le Monde Illustré Théâtral et Littéraire, 1947).

40   Duca, Lo, 'Vie et miracles du *Corbeau*', *Le Monde Illustré Théâtral et Littéraire* (4 October 1947), p. 30.

41   Duca: 'Vie et miracles du *Corbeau*', p. 31.

42   Régent, Roger, *Cinéma de France: De la fille du puisatier aux enfants du paradis* (Paris: Editions Bellefaye, 1948), p. 197.

43   Régent: *Cinéma de France: De la fille du puisatier aux enfants du paradis*, p. 198.

44   Régent: *Cinéma de France: De la fille du puisatier aux enfants du paradis*, p. 200.

45   Crowther, Bosley, 'Two French films, *Le Corbeau* and *Farrebique*, arrive at Broadway Houses', *The New York Times* (24 February 1948), p. 21.

46   NA, 'New films in London: unpleasant characters', *The Times* (8 March 1948), p. 7.

47   *Cinémonde, Le Corbeau. Le Grand Film de Pierre Fresnay* (Paris, 1950). Series *Le Film Vécu.*

48   See Mayne, Judith, 'Dora the image-maker and Henri-Georges Clouzot's *Quai des Orfèvres*', *Studies in French Cinema* 4.1 (2004), pp. 42–52.

49   See Bocquet and Godin: *Clouzot cinéaste*, p. 53.

50   Oms, Marcel, '*Le Corbeau* et ses quatre vérités', *Les Cahiers de la Cinémathèque* 8, Winter 1973, pp. 58–61.

51   Siclier: *La France de Pètain et son cinéma.*

52   Bertin-Maghit, Jean-Pierre, *Le Cinéma français sous Vichy: Les films français de 1940 à 1944* (Paris: Editions Albatros, 1980); Chirat: *Le Cinéma français des années de guerre*; Garçon, François, *De Blum à Pétain: Cinéma et Société Française (1936–1944)* (Paris: Les Editions du Cerf, 1984); Jeancolas: *15 ans d'années trente: Le cinéma des français 1929–1944* (Paris: Stock, 1983).

53   Ehrlich: *Cinema of Paradox: French Filmmaking Under the German Occupation*, p. xii.

54   Ehrlich: *Cinema of Paradox: French Filmmaking Under the German Occupation*, p. 185.

55   Burch and Sellier: *La Drôle de guerre des sexes*, pp. 191–196.

56   Sims: 'Henri-Georges Clouzot's *Le Corbeau* (1943): the work of art as will to power', pp. 743–779.

57   Bertin-Maghit: *Le Cinéma français sous l'Occupation* (1989 rpt. 2002); Bertin-Maghit, *Le Cinéma français sous l'Occupation* (1994); Bertin-Maghit, *Les Documenteurs des années noires* (Paris: Nouveau Monde Editions, 2004).

58   For a discussion of the relationship between Preminger's and Clouzot's films, see Williams, Alan, 'The Raven and the Nanny: The remake as crosscultural encounter', in *Dead Ringers: The Remake in Theory and Practice*, edited by Jennifer Forrest and Leonard Koos (Albany: SUNY Press, 2002), pp. 151–168.

Conclusion

It is rare for a single film to have the kind of influence that Marcel Ophüls's *Le Chagrin et la pitié/The Sorrow and the Pity* did in the re-evaluation of French participation in the Occupation. The film was made for French television in 1969, but was not shown until 1971 and then in theatrical release; only in 1981 was it televised in France. Lasting nearly four hours, the film challenges and demystifies the popular image of a resistant France, and focuses on the many ways in which French citizens collaborated with the enemy. The film was, to say the least, controversial, because of what it said, certainly, but also because of its extensive reliance on 'talking head' interviews – that is, on recollections by the film's subjects. The film figures prominently in Henry Rousso's *The Vichy Syndrome*, a study of the ways in which the Second World War has been repressed and remembered in France. The film is a key piece of evidence in relationship to the period 1971–1974, described by Rousso as 'The Broken Mirror' – that is, the period when new, critical interpretations of the Second World War emerged, particularly in the realms of literature and film, and when a new generation, born after the war, challenged existing versions of history.[1]

The France of the Second World War has been reconstructed in so many films, particularly since the early to mid-1970s, that they have been given a name, 'la mode rétro' (retro fashion).[2] Louis Malle's *Lacombe, Lucien* (1974) made fascism seem ordinary and accidental by focusing on the tale of a young man who seems to join the forces of the Right largely because he is turned down by the Resistance and his bicycle had a flat tyre. Michel Drach's *Les Violons du bal* (1974) was an autobiographical story about the film-maker's family encountering anti-Semitism in France during the war. The films devoted to the 1940s cover a wide range of topics and include Joseph Losey's *Monsieur Klein* (1976), François Truffaut's *Le Dernier métro/The Last Metro* (1980), Jacques Audiard's *Un héro très discret/A Self-Made Hero* (1996),

Claude Berri's *Uranus* (1990) and many more. Some of the 'retro' films are Hollywood-style dramas, like Berri's 1997 film about a married couple in the resistance, *Lucie Aubrac*; more recently, Gérard Jugnot's *Monsieur Batignole* (2002) and Jean-Paul Rappeneau's *Bon Voyage* (2003) demonstrated that the Occupation could be the occasion for farce.

Given how many films have been made about the Occupation, it is perhaps surprising that so few works have been devoted to the world of film-making during the period. There are the rare exceptions – Bernard Cohn's *Natalia* (1989) tells the story of a young Jewish actress who works in the cinema until she is deported, and *Le Plus beau pays du monde* (Marcel Bluwal, 1999) recounts the making of a film in occupied Paris. If film-making under the Occupation has not been a significant topic of choice for film-makers (neither Cohn's nor Bluwal's films received much critical attention), that changed with the appearance of Bertrand Tavernier's film *Laissez-passer* (*Safe Conduct*) in 2002. For *Laissez-passer* is a film that seeks to set the record straight on those who worked for Continental Films by suggesting that they did what they could to keep French cinema alive. One would think, then, that Clouzot would be a major player in this drama. Surprisingly, he is not.

Tavernier's film focuses on the stories of two men, Jean-Devaivre and Jean Aurenche. Both worked in the cinema of the era, Devaivre as an assistant director and Aurenche as a screenplay writer. Inspired by the memoirs of the two men, *Laissez-passer* presents their stories as representing two sides of Occupation film-making.[3] Aurenche (the eventual writing partner of Pierre Bost, who also appears in the film), is a womaniser (his love interests include an actress, a prostitute and a designer) who refuses to work for Continental on principle, until he is able to aid an out-of-luck writer by agreeing to sign on for a single film. Devaivre, married with a young child, accepts the opportunity to work at Continental with great reluctance, because of his own activities in the Resistance. Eventually Devaivre is able to use his work at Continental to gain access to secret military papers. The dramatic highlight of the film shows Devaivre, very ill with the flu, making contact with another member of the Resistance, who arranges for Devaivre to fly to England, give the papers to English officers and return to France.

The film provides a vivid portrait of film-making at Continental, and recreates scenes from films of the era including *La Main du diable*, *Au bonheur des dames* and *Douce*. Alfred Greven is an authoritarian Nazi with a humorous side (he uses a bust of Hitler as a hat rack, a detail often mentioned in descriptions of Continental's boss). Bauermeister is in charge of materials and watches over the productions like a hawk. Films had to be shot at night because of electricity shortages; food on the sets had to be protected so that hungry actors didn't eat it; films had to be completed in record time and with very few takes because of restricted resources; sets were limited because so much wood was required to make coffins for German soldiers killed in battle.

Aside from Devaivre and Aurenche, the major characters based on real people affiliated with Occupation cinema are Greven and Bauermeister, Jean-Paul Le Chanois and producer Roger Richebé. Clouzot is not entirely absent in the film, since people talk about him. When Le Chanois takes Devaivre to the Continental offices for the first time, Devaivre asks, 'What's Clouzot like?', to which Le Chanois responds: 'Difficult, but straight to the point. If you have a problem with anyone, he'll always defend you, unless you've done something stupid!' Clouzot's proposed changes to Le Chanois's screenplay for *La Main du diable* are mentioned (Devaivre rejects them). During a flashback about Le Chanois's conversations with his allies in the Communist party, a comrade dismisses *Le Corbeau* as a 'boil' and 'anti-French muck', and Le Chanois defends the film and the director.

Clouzot is there but not there in *Laissez-passer*. One suspects that Tavernier (who is a great admirer of *Le Corbeau*), in his desire to draw attention to the overall picture of French film-making (especially at Continental) during the war, downplayed Clouzot's already famous (and infamous) presence. Clouzot does appear (figuratively) in the film, as a somewhat ghostly authoritative presence at Continental. And through *Le Corbeau*, he is once again a polarising figure. *Laissez-passer* has had its own share of controversy, concerning in particular the facility with which Devaivre carries on his Resistance activities while at Continental. The film puts Clouzot and *Le Corbeau* in the background, and in so doing suggests that they are so firmly a part of Occupation history that they barely require specific mention. At the same time, the film suggests that no matter how often the story of the

Occupation is told, Clouzot and *Le Corbeau* will complicate and challenge our understandings of the nature of collaboration and resistance.

Notes

1   Rousso, Henry, *The Vichy Syndrome: History and Memory in France Since 1944* (1987; trans. Cambridge, MA and London: Harvard University Press, 1991).

2   The term 'retro mode' was not always used in a neutral way, for it describes both a fascination with the history of the 1940s as well as with its costumes and styles, leading some to assume that the evocation of the past is just a way to commodify it. See Rousso: *The Vichy Syndrome*, p. 127.

3   See Aurenche: *La Suite à l'Écran: Entretiens avec Anne et Alain Riou*; and Jean-Devaivre, *Action! Mémoires 1930–1970* (Paris: Nicolas Philippe, 2002).

Appendix 1: Credits

(Source for the credits: *L'Avant-Scène Cinéma* 186 [15 April 1977])

Le Corbeau – France, 1943

Director: Henri-Georges Clouzot
Production: Continental Films, Paris
Original screenplay: Louis Chavance
Adaptation and dialogue: Louis Chavance and Henri-Georges Clouzot
Length: 93 minutes
Began shooting 10 May 1943 at Studios Neuilly & Billancourt
Exterior shooting in the town of Monfort-Lamaury (Seine et Oise)
Distributed by Tobis
Premiered 28 September 1943

Crew:

Cinematography: Nicolas Hayer
Camera: Lemare
Sound engineer: Sivel
Music: Tony Aubain
Set decorator: André Andrejew
Assistant director: Jean Sacha
General production manager: Marcel Bryau
Production manager: Paul Polthy
Photography: Henri Pecqueux

Cast:

Doctor Rémy Germain (Doctor Germain Monatte): Pierre Fresnay
Denise: Ginette Leclerc
Doctor Vorzet: Pierre Larquey
Laura Vorzet: Micheline Francey
Marie Corbin: Héléna Manson
Rolande: Liliane Maigné

Doctor Delorme: Antoine Balpêtré
Doctor Bertrand: Louis Seigner
Saillens: Noël Roquevert
The cancer patient: Roger Blin
The mother of the cancer patient: Sylvie
The Deputy: Bernard Lancret
Bonnevi: Jean Brochard
The Assistant-Prefect: Pierre Bertin
De Maquet: Robert Clermont
Fayolles: Gustave Gallet
The notions shopkeeper: Jeanne Fusier-Gir

Appendix 2: Filmography

Henri-Georges Clouzot (1907–1977)

1942 *L'Assassin habite au 21*
1943 *Le Corbeau*
1947 *Quai des Orfèvres*
1948 *Manon*
1949 *Retour à la vie* (segment entitled '*Le Retour de Jean*')
1950 *Miquette et sa mère*
1953 *Le Salaire de la Peur*
1955 *Les Diaboliques*
1956 *Le Mystère Picasso*
1957 *Les Espions*
1960 *La Vérité*
1968 *La Prisonnière*

Selected bibliography

Aurenche, Jean, *La Suite à l'Écran: Entretiens avec Anne et Alain Riou* (Lyon: Institut Lumière/Actes Sud, 1993).

Barrot, Olivier, *L'Ecran français, 1943–1953: Histoire d'un journal et d'une èpoque* (Paris: Les éditeurs français réunis, 1979).

Bertin-Maghit, Jean-Pierre, *Le Cinéma français sous l'Occupation* (Paris: Perrin, 1989; rpt. 2002).

Bertin-Maghit, Jean-Pierre, *Le Cinéma français sous l'Occupation* (Paris: Presses Universitaires de France, 1994).

Bertin-Maghit, Jean-Pierre, *Le Cinéma français sous Vichy: Les films français de 1940 à 1944* (Paris: Editions Albatros, 1980).

Bertin-Maghit, Jean-Pierre, *Les Documenteurs des années noires* (Paris: Nouveau Monde Editions, 2004).

Bessy, Maurice and Raymond Chirat, *Histoire du cinéma français: Encyclopédie des films, 1940–1950* (Paris: Pygmalion/Gérard Watelet, 1991).

Billard, Pierre, *L'Age classique du cinéma français: Du cinéma parlant à la Nouvelle Vague* (Paris: Flammarion, 1995).

Bocquet, José-Louis, and Marc Godin, *Clouzot cinéaste* (Paris: Horizon Illimité, 2002).

Burch, Noël and Geneviève Sellier, *La Drôle de guerre des sexes du cinéma français 1930–1956* (Paris: Nathan, 1996).

Camus, Michel, 'Angèle Laval', *Les Grandes affaires criminelles*, ed. Roger Bernasconi. Vol. 9 (Geneva: Edito-Service S.A., 1975, pp. 87–1903).

Carné, Marcel with Claude Guiget, *La Vie à belles dents: Souvenirs* (Paris: J.-P. Ollivier, 1975).

Chateau, René, *Le Cinema français sous l'Occupation, 1940–1944* (Paris: Editions René Chateau, 1996).

Chavance, Louis, *Archives Scénaristiques, Le Corbeau. 1932–1938*, BIFI, Paris.

Chirat, Raymond, *Le Cinéma français des années de guerre* (Paris: Hatier/5 Continents, 1983).

Cinémonde, Le Corbeau: Le Grand Film de Pierre Fresnay (Paris, 1950). Series Le Film Vécu.

Ciupa, Karine, *Yvonne Printemps: L'Heure Bleue*, Paris: Editions Robert Laffont, 1989.

Crisp, Colin, *The Classic French Cinema* (Bloomington: Indiana University Press, 1993; rpt. 1997).

Darmon, Pierre, *Le Monde Du Cinéma Sous l'Occupation*, Paris: Stock, 1997.

Darrieux, Danielle with Jean-Pierre Ferrière, *Danielle Darrieux: Filmographie commentée par elle-même* (Paris: Editions Ramsay Cinema, 1995).

Dubeux, Albert, *Pierre Fresnay* (Paris: Calmann-Lévy, 1950).

Duchâteau, André-Paul, and Stéphane Steeman, *L'Écrivain habite au 21: Stanislas-André Steeman* (Ottignies, Belgium: Quorum, 1998).

Ehrlich, Evelyn, *Cinema of Paradox: French Filmmaking Under the German Occupation* (New York: Columbia University Press, 1985).

Feuillère, Edwige, *Les Feux de la mémoire* (Paris: Albin Michel, 1977).

Fresnay, Pierre and François Possot, *Pierre Fresnay* (Paris: Editions de la Table Ronde, 1975).

Garçon, François, *De Blum à Pétain: Cinéma et Société Française, 1936–1944*. Paris: Les Editions du Cerf, 1984.

Gilles, Christian, *Ginette Leclerc: Le Désir Des Hommes* (Paris: L'Harmattan, 2000).

Halimi, André, *La Délation sous l'Occupation* (Paris: Alain Moreau, 1983).

Hayward, Susan, *Les Diaboliques* (London: I.B.Tauris, 2005).

Hayward, Susan, *French National Cinema* (London and New York: Routledge, 1993).

Jackson, Julian, *France: The Dark Years, 1940–1944* (Oxford and New York: Oxford University Press, 2001).

Jean-Devaivre, *Action! Mémoires 1930–1970* (Paris: Nicolas Philippe, 2002).

Jeancolas, Jean-Pierre, *15 ans d'années trente: Le cinéma des français 1929–1944* (Paris: Stock, 1983).

Lacourbe, Roland, *Henri-Georges Clouzot. Anthologie du cinema* no. 94, in *L'Avant-scène cinema* no. 186 (15 April 1977).

Lagny, Michèle, 'Les Français en focalisation interne', *Iris* 2 (1984), pp. 85–98.

Leclerc, Ginette, *Ma vie privée* (Paris: Editions de la Table Ronde, 1963).

Le Naour, Jean, *Le Corbeau: Histoire vraie d'une rumeur* (Paris: Hachette Littératures, 2006).

Locard, Edmond, *Les Anonymographes* (Brussels: Ferdinand Larcier, 1923).

Locard, Edmond, 'L'affaire de Tulle: Un Cas typique d'anonymographie', *L'Avenir Médical* 20.7 (July–August 1923), pp. 3–7.

Locard, Edmond, *Mémoires d'un criminologiste* (Paris: Librairie Arthème Fayard, 1958).

Locard, Edmond, *La Vipère* (Paris: Editions de la flamme d'or, 1954).

Mayne, Judith, 'Dora the image-maker and Henri-Georges Clouzot's *Quai Des Orfèvres*', *Studies in French Cinema* 4.1 (2004), pp. 42–52.

Muel-Dreyfus, Francine, *Vichy et l'éternel féminin* (Paris: Editions du Seuil, 1996).

Mulvey, Laura, 'Visual pleasure and narrative cinema', *Screen* 16.3 (Autumn 1975), pp. 6–18.

Oms, Marcel, '*Le Corbeau* et ses quatre vérités', *Les Cahiers de la Cinémathèque* 8 (Winter 1973), pp. 58–61.

Paxton, Robert, *Vichy France: Old Guard and New Order, 1940–1944* (New York: Columbia University Press, 1972).

Pithon, Rémy, 'Cinéma français et cinéma allemand des années trente: de l'échange à l'exil', *Entre Locarno et Vichy: Les Relations Culturelles Franco-Allemandes dans les Années 1930*, ed. Hans Manfred Bock, Reinhart Meyer-Kalkus and Michel Trebitsch (Paris: CNRS Editions, 1993) pp. 587–599.

Pollard, Miranda, *Reign of Virtue: Mobilizing Women in Vichy France* (Chicago: University of Chicago Press, 1998).

Ragache, Gilles, and Jean-Robert Ragache, *La Vie quotidienne des écrivains et des artistes sous l'Occupation, 1940–1944.* (Paris: Hachette, 1988).

Rebatet, Lucien, *Les Tribus du cinéma et du théatre* (Paris: Nouvelles Editions Françaises, 1941).

Régent, Roger, *Cinéma de France: De la fille du puisatier aux enfants du paradis* (Paris: Editions Bellefaye, 1948).

Richebé, Roger. *Au-Delà de l'Écran: 70 ans de la vie d'un cinéaste* (Monte-Carlo: Editions Pastorelly, 1977).

Rousso, Henry, *The Vichy Syndrome: History and Memory in France Since 1944* (Cambridge, MA and London: Harvard University Press, 1991).

Schwengler, Olivier, '*Le Corbeau*', *CinémAction* 103 (2002), pp. 44–50.

Semple, Jeanie, 'Ambiguities in the film Le Ciel est à vous', *Vichy France and the Resistance: Culture and Ideology*, ed. Roderick Kedward and Roger Austin (London and Sydney: Croom Helm, 1985), pp. 123–132.

Siclier, Jacques, *La France de Pétain et son cinéma* (Paris: Editions Henri Veyrier, 1981).

Sims, Gregory, 'Henri-Georges Clouzot's *Le Corbeau* (1943): the work of art as will to power', *MLN* (*Modern Language Notes*) 11.4 (1999), pp. 743–779.

Sweets, John F., *Choices in Vichy France* (New York and Oxford: Oxford University Press, 1986).

Tarr, Carrie, 'Wilful Women in French Cinema Under the German Occupation'. *Women and Representation*, ed. Diana Knight and Judith Still. Nottingham, England: Women Teaching French Occasional Papers (3), 1995, pp. 75–91.

Thalmann, Rita, *La Mise Au Pas: Idéologie et Stratégie Sécuritaire dans la France Occupée* (Paris: Fayard, 1991).

Vincendeau, Ginette, 'French film noir', *European Film Noir*, ed. Andrew Spicer (Manchester: Manchester University Press, 2007), pp. 23-54.

Vincendeau, Ginette, *Pépé le Moko* (London: British Film Institute, 1998).

Virgili, Fabrice, *La France 'virile': Des Femmes tondues à la libération* (Paris: Editions Payot et Rivages, 2000; rpt. 2004)

Williams, Alan, *Republic of Images: A History of French Filmmaking* (Cambridge, MA and London: Harvard University Press, 1992)

Williams, Alan, 'The Raven and the Nanny: The remake as crosscultural encounter', *Dead Ringers: The Remake in Theory and Practice*, ed. Jennifer Forrest and Leonard Koos (Albany: SUNY Press, 2002), pp. 151–168.

Index